THE PAPACY

STEPHEN K. RAY and R. DENNIS WALTERS

The Papacy

*What the Pope Does and
Why It Matters*

IGNATIUS PRESS   SAN FRANCISCO

Cover art and design by Enrique J. Aguilar

© 2018 by Ignatius Press, San Francisco
All rights reserved
ISBN 978-1-62164-216-9
Library of Congress Control Number 2018931265
Printed in the United States of America ∞

CONTENTS

Chapter 1

The Papacy and You

You are walking along the narrow streets of Jerusalem. Suddenly, you hear a rushing wind and you look around in surprise. A crowd is gathering around a group of men preaching, and everyone is talking excitedly. You run to see what is happening, and you discover that the men preaching, though simple Galileans, are declaring God's wonders in every language that you—a world traveler— have ever encountered. How strange!

What you experienced was Pentecost—the promised Holy Spirit of God coming down to dwell in the hearts of men, giving birth to the Church. What happened after Pentecost? What did everybody do next? Hypothetically, they might have done a number of things.

First everyone *might* have received the Holy Spirit and simply returned home on fire with love for God and Temple worship. The apostles too might have gone home and devoted their lives to personal prayer and meditation. If so, the new Christian movement might have begun and ended within one generation.

Second the apostles *might* have divided the crowd into groups, each explaining from his own point of view what had just happened, and encouraging his group to be baptized and receive the promised Holy Spirit. The groups might then have scattered to faraway countries and spread the news of the gospel. The apostles might have independently traveled to foreign lands and established churches, setting themselves up as leaders. But with no central authority, these various churches might have understood the gospel in culturally diverse and conflicting ways. Competing groups might have sprung up, dividing Christians into sects, each saying it had the truth and condemning the others as heretics. In this scenario, the pagan empire might have swallowed up Christianity in a matter of a few centuries.

Third, Peter, as the leader of the apostles, might have explained to the crowd what was going on, linking the descent of the Holy Spirit with Jesus' recent death and Resurrection, and urging his hearers to repent and be baptized so they could receive the Spirit, too. The thousands that would believe in Christ would have gathered together and devoted themselves to the teaching of the apostles, fellowship, the breaking of the bread (Eucharist), and the prayers (Acts 2:14–42). Christianity would have spread to all parts of the known world, turning the whole Roman Empire upside down for Jesus within four centuries. Peter and his successors would provide leadership and unity in the universal Church. And the assembly that began with Peter's speech would have kept growing—and the gates of hell would not prevail against it (Mt 16:18).

Of course, the third possibility is just what *did* happen. So what does that mean for *us* today—for *you*?

A Divine Pattern of Leadership

The early believers gathered together. They did it spontaneously. And they did it everywhere the gospel was preached. Nowhere do you find scriptural accounts of

Christian loners, solitary believers wandering off on their own, rugged individualists privately hugging their new faith while rejecting Church authority. There were no "Just Jesus and me" believers.

Quite the opposite. "The company of those who believed were of one heart and soul" (Acts 4:32)—a way of indicating how intimate the grouping was. "All these with one accord devoted themselves to prayer, together with the women and Mary the mother of Jesus" (Acts 1:14). Faith was personal but not private, and the natural response of new believers was to share it. Whole households—parents, children, extended family members, and even servants— were baptized together. The first group met often, worshipped together in Solomon's Portico of the Temple (Acts 5:12), held everything in common, and shared what they had with believers in need (Acts 4:34).

As multitudes were added in increasing numbers (Acts 5:14), questions arose about how to take care of everyone. The Twelve realized the need to develop structures of care and service to complement their work of preaching and teaching (Acts 6:1–7). And as the faith spread outward, people kept doing what they had started doing, gathering in groups called *churches*.

Jesus had referred to what he would build as "my Church" (Mt 16:18). We have the word from the Greek *ekklesia*, which, as the *Catechism of the Catholic Church* points out, "means a convocation or an assembly" (*CCC* 751). We tend to think of an assembly as a meeting with a scheduled agenda. To ancient Jews and the early Christians, however, an *ekklesia* was much more than this. From the beginning, they lived life with God as part of a group.

They were following a scriptural pattern. In the Old Testament, God blessed the Israelites by giving them a covenant, a kind of sacred agreement that in effect creates a family. When two persons marry, they make a covenant that says what they will be for each other, in essence: "I will be your husband"; "I will be your wife." When God made his covenant with the Chosen People, he said: "I will be your God, and you shall be my people" (Jer 7:23; cf. Lev 26:12; Ezek 36:28). Some people in the Old Testament knew God personally—as Abraham and Moses did—but the average Israelite related to God through the covenant family. To belong to the family of God was life; to be cut off from it brought death. No Israelite wanted to be cut off.

When it came to the People of God, there was a structure. The group related to God through an individual who acted as a mediator between them and God. When God sent Moses to Egypt to lead his people out of "the house of bondage" (Ex 13:3), Moses became the person everyone looked to. Under God's direction, Moses led them through the Red Sea, through desert sands, to Sinai. And there, when God manifested his presence on the mountain in thunder, lightning, dense cloud, and loud trumpet blasts, the terrified people begged Moses not to let God speak to them directly. "You speak to us, and we will hear; but let not God speak to us, lest we die" (Ex 20:19).

It was an arrangement that God approved and continued to use in the future with the prophets (Deut 18:15–19). So Moses became the representative, speaking to God for the people and teaching the people what God expected of them.

Moses led the Israelites as God directed. As long as they listened to God through Moses, things went well with the Israelites; but when they failed to listen—or took matters into their own hands (Num 16)—disaster struck. When the time came for Moses to die, he handed his office to Joshua (cf. Num 27:15–23). After Joshua's time, the leadership of God's people passed through the hands of many judges, but there remained a leader. In the time of Jesus, the leader was the High Priest.

The leader also had assistants. The Israelite kings had an assistant known as a vizier, or "chief steward", whose office was symbolized by holding "the key of the house of David" (Is 22:22; Rev 3:7). When Hezekiah's chief steward, a vizier named Shebna, failed in his office, Isaiah warned that God would give his key to a successor named Eliakim, saying, "And I will place on his shoulder the key of the house of David; he shall open, and none shall shut; and he shall shut, and none shall open" (Is 22:22).

In building the Church on Peter (whose name means "rock") and giving him the keys of the kingdom (Mt 16:18–19), Jesus continued God's method of relating to his people through a leader (see Scripture and the Pattern of Leadership on p. 12). Peter took up the keys, and he began shutting some doors and opening others—governing the Church.

He opened one door by resisting pressure to restrict Christianity to circumcised Jews (Acts 11:1–18). Given a vision that challenged everything he knew about contact with "the unclean", Peter opened the doors of salvation and baptism to the uncircumcised Gentiles (Acts 10). He then guided the Jerusalem council to admit non-Jews into the Church without the need for circumcision (Acts 15:8–12). Peter also guided daily Church life, regulating the distribution of donated property (Acts 5:1–11) and the sacraments, such as baptism (Acts 10:47–48) and confirmation (Acts 8:14–24). He was exercising the keys as the chief steward of God's kingdom.

Once again, the pattern was set, this time among Christians: God speaks to the Church through Peter. In two letters, Peter addresses churches. In these letters, he urges proper conduct in society and in the family, and encourages his readers to accept the "fiery ordeal" of persecution (1 Pet 4:12). He stresses virtue and warns against unsound

Scripture and the Pattern of Leadership

Isaiah about Eliakim: "In that day I will call my servant Eliakim the son of Hilkiah, and I will clothe him with your robe, and will bind your belt on him, and will commit your authority to his hand; and he shall be a father to the inhabitants of Jerusalem and to the house of Judah. And I will place on his shoulder the key of the house of David; he shall open, and none shall shut; and he shall shut, and none shall open. And I will fasten him like a peg in a sure place, and he will become a throne of honor to his father's house." (Is 22:20–23)

Jesus to Simon: "Blessed are you, Simon Bar-Jona! For flesh and blood has not revealed this to you, but my Father who is in heaven. And I tell you, you are Peter, and on this rock I will build my Church, and the gates of Hades shall not prevail against it. I will give you the keys of the kingdom of heaven, and whatever you bind on earth shall be bound in heaven, and whatever you loose on earth shall be loosed in heaven." (Mt 16:17–19)

doctrine. We know from early Church history that Peter appointed successors. His third successor, Clement of Rome, acted as Peter did, by instructing the Christians of Corinth that they could not depose their bishops.

Through our baptism, the Holy Spirit invites us into the family of God. He does not mean for us to be solitary individuals. Jesus is the head of a Body, his Church, and our membership in it makes each of us "members one of another" (Rom 12:5; cf. 1 Cor 10:17; 12:20, 27; Eph 4:25). The spiritual gifts we exercise are intended for the good of the Body (1 Cor 12:7), and are subject to the oversight of the Church's shepherds (*CCC* 801). Jesus told Peter that he was to "feed my sheep" (Jn 21:17; cf. 21:15–16), and to "strengthen your brethren" (Lk 22:32), which in this case was referring especially to Peter's leadership of his fellow apostles. He also promised that the Holy Spirit, the Spirit of truth, would lead the Church into "all the truth" (Jn 16:13). The charism of infallibility is the Spirit's guarantee that through the pope the Church is reliably hearing what the Spirit himself speaks (*CCC* 891) and passing it on (see Papal Infallibility below).

Vatican Council I Defines Papal Infallibility *1870*

"The Roman Pontiff, when he speaks ex cathedra†, that is, when acting in the office of shepherd and teacher of all Christians, he defines, by virtue of his supreme apostolic authority, a doctrine concerning faith or morals to be held by the universal Church, possesses through the divine assistance promised to him in the person of Blessed Peter, the infallibility with which the divine Redeemer willed his Church to be endowed in defining the doctrine concerning faith or morals; and that such definitions of the Roman Pontiff are therefore irreformable of themselves, not because of the consent of the Church." (Vatican Council I, *Pastor Aeternus* [July 18, 1870], in *Decree of Damasus* 3, in Joseph Neuner, S.J., and Jacques Dupuis, *The Christian Faith in the Doctrinal Documents of the Catholic Church*, 7th rev. ed. [New York: Alba House, 2001], pp. 321–22)

The pattern begun long ago continues into the present. The pope transmits the Christian faith to the modern world as he has throughout the ages, feeding and governing God's family.

How the Papacy Affects You

So, what does a pope in far-off Rome have to do with you and me? The pope's leadership colors everything about the faith we profess, and the way we live it. Here are a few examples among hundreds from history, including some demonstrating that the pope's leadership occasionally extends beyond faith and morals.

As for faith, our belief in the human and divine natures of Jesus rests in part on the intervention of Pope Saint Leo I (440–461) in the form of a long letter to Flavian, patriarch of Constantinople, written in 449 (known as the Tome of Leo). Leo's Tome explained how the Church's faith in Jesus held that he was one person with two natures—human and divine. Two years later, the Tome was accepted during the meeting of bishops at the Council of Chalcedon (in modern Turkey), when the bishops applauded his explanation by shouting, "Peter has spoken through Leo."[1]

Papal definitions confirmed and clarified long-standing beliefs about Mary. For centuries most Catholics believed that Mary was immaculately conceived and assumed body and soul into heaven, though some individual theologians disagreed. Two popes settled these matters. Based on apostolic Tradition and the faith of the Church over the

[1] For further information, see the section in chapter 4 that discusses Saint Leo the Great.

centuries, in 1854 Pius IX defined the Immaculate Conception of Mary as divinely revealed. In 1950, Pius XII defined the Assumption of Mary into heaven as a matter of revelation on the same grounds—the faith of the Church and apostolic Tradition (see Marian Doctrines below).

The Popes Define Marian Doctrines Infallibly

The Immaculate Conception: "The most Blessed Virgin Mary was, from the first moment of her conception, by a singular grace and privilege of almighty God and in view of the merits of Jesus Christ, Savior of the human race, preserved immune from all stain of original sin." (Pius IX, Apostolic Constitution on the Immaculate Conception *Ineffabilis Deus* [Ineffable God] [December 8, 1854], in Joseph Neuner, S.J., and Jacques Dupuis, *The Christian Faith in the Doctrinal Documents of the Catholic Church*, 7th rev. ed. [New York: Alba House, 2001], p. 284)

The Assumption: "Finally the Immaculate Virgin, preserved free from all stain of original sin, when the course of her earthly life was finished, was taken up body and soul into heavenly glory, and exalted by the Lord as Queen over all things, so that she might be the more fully conformed to her Son, the Lord of lords and conqueror of sin and death." (Pius XII, *Munificentissimus Deus* [November 1, 1950], in Denzinger-Schënmetzer, *Enchridion Symbolorum, definitionum et declarationum de rebus fidei et morum* 3903 [Freiburg: Herder, 1965])

As for the moral life, popes from the first century onward have defended Catholic moral teaching against the errors of their times. In recent times they have had to

- promote chastity within marriage and openness to the transmission of life (Pius XI, *Casti Connubi* [December 31, 1930]; Paul VI, *Humanae Vitae* [July 25, 1968]; John Paul II, *Evangelium Vitae* [March 25, 1995]; Francis in various remarks to the media);
- champion the right of workers to earn a living wage and to form labor unions (Leo XIII);
- urge rich nations to ensure a just distribution of wealth with poorer nations (John XXIII, *Pacem in Terris* [April 11, 1963]; Paul VI, *Populorum Progressio* [March 26, 1967]; John Paul II, *Laborem Exercens* [September 14, 1981], *Sollicitudo Rei Socialis* [December 30, 1987], *Centesimus Annus* [May 1, 1991]);
- defend the sanctity of the human person (all modern popes, especially John Paul II, *Evangelium Vitae* [March 25,1995]); and
- uphold Catholic moral teaching as objective truth (John Paul II, *Veritatis Splendor* [August 6, 1993]).

Papal teaching extends to matters of faith and morals, but popes also make decisions regarding Church discipline that affect the daily lives of Catholics everywhere:

- When an exaggerated sense of unworthiness kept Catholics from receiving the Eucharist, Pius X urged frequent reception of Communion in *Quam Singulari* (August 8, 1910).
- In *Divino Afflante Spiritus* (September 30, 1943), Pius XII spurred Catholic scholars to study the original languages of the Bible, promoted fresh translations of

Scripture, and encouraged lay Catholics to read and study Scripture.

- Pius XII also revised the Holy Week liturgy to the form we know today in *De Solemni Vigilia Paschali Instauranda* (February 9, 1951). After the Second Vatican Council, Pope Blessed Paul VI promulgated revised rites for the celebration of the sacraments in an *Apostolic Constitution Missale Romanum* (April 3, 1969).

- Papal contacts with leaders of other Christian communions have led to a new age of ecumenism and cooperation between Catholics and their fellow Christians. (See, for example, Joint Statement by Pope Francis and Towardros II, April 28, 2017.)

Papal leadership even extends into secular areas. Our Gregorian calendar is named after Pope Gregory XIII (1572–1585), who adjusted it to synchronize dates with seasons (the old Julian calendar was ten days off). The Pontifical Academy of Sciences includes renowned scientists from all over the world. The Holy See maintains diplomatic relations with countries everywhere, including the United States. Statesmen still ask the pope to help settle disputes among nations. And Pope Saint John Paul II played a key role in the downfall of Communism in Poland and the rest of Europe.

The Papacy—a Principle of Unity

To Mark Twain, Christianity was unbelievable because of its many divisions, each group claiming to possess the truth and each contradicting the others. Characteristically using exaggeration to make a point, Twain suggested that, in a "scientific experiment", if Christians of different persuasions were caged in the same room overnight, they would tear each other apart by morning. If he were alive today, Twain would surely comment on the accelerating divisions. According to the *World Christian Encyclopedia* there are many thousands of different denominations in the world today.[2] The Church, the Body of Christ, was *certainly* not meant to be fractured in this way, any more than a body is meant to be torn apart (1 Cor 1:10).

Christians of all persuasions often admire the pope as a symbol of unity, morality, and stability. He represents something they yearn for—"That they may be one even as we are one, I in them and you in me, that they may become perfectly one, so that the world may know that you have sent me" (Jn 17:22–23).

Christian unity is a sign that Jesus is for real (see Sign of Unity on p. 19).

But papal leadership has not always been easy even for Catholics to accept. Sometimes the pope makes tough decisions that are unpopular or hard to understand. Many cardinals in 1959 opposed holding an ecumenical council, but Pope Saint John XXIII called one anyway.[3] Many Catholics were disappointed when Paul VI confirmed traditional Church teaching on contraception, but he did.[4]

---

[2] David B. Barrett, George Thomas Kurian, and Todd M. Johnson, *World Christian Encyclopedia: A Comparative Survey of Churches and Religions in the Modern World*, 2nd ed., vol. 1, *The World by Countries: Religionists, Churches, Ministries* (New York: Oxford University Press, 2001), p. 16.

[3] In January 1959, only a few months after his election in October 1958, Pope John XXIII announced his intention of convening a council. He opened the Second Vatican Council in 1962. See https://en.wikipedia.org/wiki/Second_Vatican_Council.

[4] See Paul VI, Encyclical Letter on the Regulation of Birth *Humanae Vitae* (July 25, 1968), http://w2.vatican.va/content/paul-vi/en/encyclicals/documents/hf_p-vi_enc_25071968_humanae-vitae.html.

The Pope as a Sign of Unity

Quoting the Vatican II document *Lumen Gentium*, the *Catechism of the Catholic Church* says: "The Pope, Bishop of Rome and Peter's successor, 'is the perpetual and visible source and foundation of the unity both of the bishops and of the whole company of the faithful' (*LG* 23). 'For the Roman Pontiff, by reason of his office as Vicar of Christ, and as pastor of the entire Church has full, supreme, and universal power over the whole Church, a power which he can always exercise unhindered' (*LG* 22)." (*CCC* 882)

Pope John Paul II began a tradition of tremendously successful World Youth Days, even though some initially thought a cynical youth culture would boycott them.[5]

The fact is that without the pope's divinely guided leadership, the Church would suffer the fragmentation and contradictions that many Christian groups know firsthand. Without his leadership, the one, holy, catholic, and apostolic Church that Jesus intended would break apart. Holiness would be a distant (or ignored) ideal, factions would trample unity, and the teaching passed down from the apostles would be subject to arbitrary, relative, and numerous interpretations. The Bark of Peter would smash on the rocks, and Catholics would drift away from Jesus Christ on secular currents.

In this book, we will look at the papacy from different angles. Chapters 2 and 3 examine the pope's roles as leader

[5] For additional information about World Youth Day, see their website at http://worldyouthday.com/.

and teacher of the truth. Chapter 4 tells the stories of several men who became great popes. Chapter 5 describes how a pope is selected, and how the election process developed. Because the pope is not for Catholics only, chapter 6 explains how he is important for other Christian and even non-Christian groups. Chapter 7 answers some of the most common attacks on the papacy by anti-Catholics. Chapter 8 ends this study by showing how we relate to the pope in our own lives.

For a comprehensive chronological list of popes, a short glossary of technical terms used in this book, and some sources where more can be learned, see the appendixes provided.

Chapter 2

The Pope as Leader

Catholics are more than a *billion* strong in the world. That's a lot of people! Catholicism is by far the largest Christian body in the world. In the United States alone Catholics currently number roughly 20 percent of the total U.S. population.[1]

Impressive numbers? You bet! But they raise an important question: How have *so* many Catholics from *so* many cultures been *so* unified for *so* many centuries?

The Pope as the Servant of God's Servants

Of course, the Church wasn't always so large. The kingdom of heaven is like a tiny mustard seed that grew into a tree large enough for birds to nest in (Mt 13:31–32).

After the first Pentecost, the Church's organization was simple. Peter and the apostles could handle almost everything. When Christians became more numerous, these leaders appointed deacons to handle certain tasks (Acts 6). Later, they also appointed "elders" or presbyters (Acts

---

[1] "America's Changing Religious Landscape", Pew Research Center: Religion and Public Life, May 12, 2015, www.pewforum.org/2015/05/12/americas-changing-religious-landscape/.

14:23), the Greek term from which we derive the word "priests". They also appointed bishops to oversee the churches in each locality. New churches grew up all over the Roman Empire with the same basic leadership structure. For the first two or three hundred years, churches were small enough to be cared for by a bishop, some presbyters, and the deacons—a three-tiered structure.

Papal authority was exercised only when required (see Newman on Papal Leadership on p. 23). That is not to say that some kind of papal leadership was not present, only that it was exercised in special circumstances.

As we see from Acts, Peter's authority had three facets: governing, teaching, and sanctifying the Church. Each of these is reflected in Peter's power of the keys. This "power of the keys", says the *Catechism*, gives him "authority to absolve sins, to pronounce doctrinal judgments, and to make disciplinary decisions in the Church" (*CCC* 553). Let's take a look at each aspect.

First, *governing*. When Jesus gave Peter the keys of the kingdom of heaven with power to bind and to loose (Mt 16:19), he gave him legal and moral authority.[2] Equipped with this authority, Peter opened the door of baptism to the Gentiles. Later he defended his actions as directed by the Holy Spirit (Acts 10). When the question came up again, Peter directed the Council of Jerusalem to bypass circumcision for the Gentiles, a pronouncement that was binding upon all the churches (Acts 15:6–12) (see Peter Speaks on p. 24).

Peter realized the Twelve needed a successor to Judas Iscariot and conducted the election (Acts 1:15–22). He

---

[2] Cf. Stephen K. Ray, *Upon This Rock: St. Peter and the Primacy of Rome in Scripture and the Early Church*, Modern Apologetics Library (San Francisco: Ignatius Press, 1999), p. 42n54.

Newman on the Development of Papal Leadership

"While apostles were on earth, there was the display neither of bishop nor pope; their power had no prominence, as being exercised by apostles. In course of time, first the power of the bishop displayed itself, and then the power of the pope....

"This is but natural, and is parallel to instances which happen daily.... St. Peter's prerogative would remain a mere letter till the complication of ecclesiastical matters became the cause of ascertaining it....

"When the Church, then, was thrown upon her own resources, first local disturbances gave exercise to bishops, and next ecumenical disturbances gave exercise to popes; and whether communion with the pope was necessary for Catholicity would not and could not be debated till a suspension of that communion had actually occurred.

"It is not a greater difficulty that St. Ignatius [of Antioch] does not write to the Asian Greeks about popes than that St. Paul does not write to the Corinthians about bishops. And it is a less difficulty that the papal supremacy was not formally acknowledged in the second century than that there was no formal acknowledgment on the part of the Church of the doctrine of the Holy Trinity till the fourth. No doctrine is defined till it is violated." (John Henry Newman, *An Essay on the Development of Christian Doctrine*, in *Conscience, Consensus, and the Development of Doctrine*, ed. James Gaffney [New York: Doubleday Image Books, 1992], pp. 157–58) organized the Jerusalem community and passed judgment on its members: Ananias and Sapphira fell dead at his feet when they deceived the community (Acts 4:32—5:11). With John, Peter confirmed the Samaritan Christians (Acts 8:14–17). He approved Paul's ministry to the Gentiles (Gal 2:6–10), and exhorted fellow elders to tend the churches in their care as he himself did (1 Pet 5:1–2).

Peter Speaks at the Council of Jerusalem

"But some believers who belonged to the party of the Pharisees rose up, and said, 'It is necessary to circumcise [the Gentiles], and to charge them to keep the law of Moses.'

"The apostles and the elders were gathered together to consider this matter. And after there had been much debate, Peter rose and said to them, 'Brethren, you know that in the early days God made choice among you, *that by my mouth* the Gentiles should hear the word of the gospel and believe. And God who knows the heart bore witness to them, giving them the Holy Spirit just as he did to us; and he made no distinction between us and them, but cleansed their hearts by faith. Now therefore why do you make trial of God by putting a yoke upon the neck of the disciples which neither our fathers nor we have been able to bear? But we believe that we shall be saved through the grace of the Lord Jesus, just as they will.'

"And all the assembly kept silence." (Acts 15:5–12; emphasis added)

Second, *teaching*. Jesus told Peter that he was to "feed my sheep" (Jn 21:17), which involved a teaching role. So, on Pentecost Peter explained the good news to pilgrims in Jerusalem (Acts 2). Peter announced, in front of the Jewish ruling council, the Sanhedrin, that salvation comes only through the name of Jesus (Acts 4:12). Under Peter, the earliest Christians learned the apostolic teaching (Acts 2:42; 4:33; 5:42). As their chief teacher, Peter faced arrest and imprisonment (Acts 4—5:12). And, when he was older, he expressed a concern that his teaching continue after him (2 Pet 1:12–15).

Third, *sanctifying*. When thousands responded on Pentecost and received the Holy Spirit, Peter and the other apostles baptized and instructed them (Acts 2:41). He healed people in the public streets (Acts 5:15–16) and raised a dead woman to life (Acts 9:32–43). He headed the community, coordinated the distribution of alms, and instituted the diaconate (Acts 2:44; 6:1–6). Peter's whole purpose was that the Church might grow in holiness (1 Pet 2:9; 2 Pet 3:11–14).

But the Church did not remain small, and as she grew so did the exercise of papal authority. The authority of the office became well established, and early on only a few decisions were challenged.

The bishop of Rome's authority extended into all three of the foregoing areas. In *governing*, the third pope (Clement) had to decide an important matter in the Church at Corinth: Could the local church depose bishops who had been properly ordained and appointed? (Interestingly, the Corinthians did not appeal to the Apostle John, presumably still alive and residing in nearby Ephesus, but to Clement in faraway Rome). Clement replied that they could not, and that those deposed should be reinstated (see Clement of Rome on p. 26).

Clement of Rome to the Corinthians, on Deposing Bishops

"Our Apostles, too, were given to understand by our Lord Jesus Christ that the office of the bishop would give rise to intrigues. For this reason, equipped as they were with perfect foreknowledge, they appointed the men mentioned before, and afterwards laid down a rule once for all to this effect: when these men die, other approved men shall succeed to their sacred ministry.

"Consequently, we deem it an injustice to eject from the sacred ministry the persons who were appointed either by them, or later, with the consent of the whole Church, by other men in high repute and have ministered to the flock of Christ faultlessly, humbly, quietly and unselfishly, and have moreover, over a long period of time, earned the esteem of all.

"Indeed, it will be no small sin for us if we oust men who have irreproachably and piously offered the sacrifices proper to the episcopate." (Clement of Rome and Ignatius of Antioch, *The Epistles of St. Clement of Rome and St. Ignatius of Antioch*, ed. Johannes Quasten and Joseph C. Plumpe, trans. James A. Kleist, *Ancient Christian Writers*, 1st ed. [New York: Paulist Press, 1946], p. 36)

Although couched in kindly language, Clement's authoritative letter expects obedience: "But should any disobey what has been said by Him through us, let them understand that they will entangle themselves in transgression and no small danger."[3] Less than a century later, Pope Saint Victor I (189–199) exercised the authority to set a common date for Easter and to excommunicate any churches that resisted. Though some, like Saint Irenaeus of Lyons, disagreed with this move and counseled leniency (and Victor did relent), no one questioned the bishop of Rome's right to exercise such authority.

In *teaching*, Rome's devotion to the apostolic Tradition earned the respect of the Christian world. Early development of basic doctrines led to all sorts of confusion, even among bishops, some teaching one thing and some another. Some authority had to define true Christian doctrine. Because of Rome's singular authority and recognized orthodoxy, parties on all sides appealed to the bishop of Rome to settle doctrinal matters. The popes displayed a clear awareness of their right and duty to intervene, as Pope Saint Leo I did at the Council of Chalcedon.

In *sanctifying*, the power of binding and loosing applied to the development of liturgical worship in the early Church. Popes defended the validity of baptism properly administered by heretics and granted forgiveness to apostates desiring to return to the Church. Peter's martyrdom at Rome became the standard of witness among all the popes. Many popes of the first three centuries were martyrs; but even if they were not killed outright, they often underwent imprisonment, exile, and persecution for Christ. The popes willingly laid down their lives for the Church, following the examples of Jesus and Peter.

What does the exercise of papal authority mean? From one perspective, the pope is a bishop among bishops. As

[3] Clement of Rome and Ignatius of Antioch, *The Epistles of St. Clement of Rome and St. Ignatius of Antioch*, ed. Johannes Quasten and Joseph C. Plumpe, trans. James A. Kleist, *Ancient Christian Writers*, 1st ed. (New York: Paulist Press, 1946), 45.

a bishop, he has the same sacramental authority as other bishops to govern, to teach, and to sanctify. But because the pope succeeds to the office of Peter, he enjoys a kind of "firstness" or *primacy* that puts him at the head of all other bishops. So far, so good. For roughly the first thousand years, everyone agreed on that much. But the Church grew in size and complexity, the political center of the Roman Empire shifted eastward, and the cultural and religious distance between the East and the West widened. In the course of time, two very different views emerged of what papal primacy meant.

The position held by many Eastern Orthodox churches today contradicts that of the early Fathers. These churches tend to hold that the bishop of Rome enjoys a primacy of honor, but not of authority—Peter the "rock" was head of the apostles, sure, but his headship was a matter of prominence and dignity, not of authority. The phrase "primacy of honor" is often used today to minimize the role of Rome. However, the phrase implied much more in the first millennium than the minimalized view held by some in the East today. Early Eastern Fathers certainly held to a primacy of authority, among them Saint Flavian, Saint Maximus the Confessor, Saint Ephraim, and Saint Theodore the Studite.

It's true that, in the East, bishops tended to be more interested in the inner life of their churches than in their structure. Communications with other bishops were inclined to be fraternal and collegial rather than juridical. Bishops made decisions in synods, as a group, as the Council of Jerusalem did (Acts 15). However, the fact that patriarchs from Constantinople, Alexandria, Antioch, and Jerusalem submitted disputes to Rome for resolution meant they trusted Rome to hold faithfully to the Tradition of the apostles and had the authority to make final decisions.

According to the West, the pope has always enjoyed a primacy of both honor and authority; Christ commissioned Peter to govern, teach, and sanctify the *whole* Church. Based on Scripture and Tradition, the West recognized that papal primacy included unique authority—authority to rule. Rule meant jurisdiction, and jurisdiction meant oversight of other bishops, including patriarchs, and of ecumenical councils. As time passed, the word *jurisdiction* appeared more and more often in discussions about the papal role.

Slowly over the course of time, the Eastern churches drifted away from the West and, despite their previous theory and practice, rejected the pope's primacy of jurisdiction. Most abandoned communion with Rome after the turn of the second millennium—though some never left and others returned to full communion later.

The Second Vatican Council discussed the relationship between the pope and other bishops. Vatican II documents emphasize collegiality. They stress that bishops govern, teach, and sanctify as a college, with the pope at its head. The documents also avoid terms like *jurisdiction* when describing the papal role. Instead, they refer to the pope's " 'full, supreme, and universal power over the whole Church' (*LG* 22)" (*CCC* 882). While the pope does exercise the power of jurisdiction over the whole Church, popes since Paul VI have preferred to use terms like "primacy of service", "pastoral power", and "ministry".[4]

[4] See John Paul II, "The Pope Exercises Supreme Jurisdiction", General Audience (February 24, 1993), http://totus2us.com/vocation/jpii-catechesis -on-the-church/the-pope-exercises-supreme-jurisdiction/. Also, John Paul II, *Ut Unum Sint* (May 25, 1995), nos. 95–97, http://w2.vatican.va/content/john -paul-ii/en/encyclicals/documents/hf_jp-ii_enc_25051995_ut-unum-sint .html#%2449. Cf. Joseph Ratzinger (Pope Benedict XVI), "Homily at the Mass [for the] Imposition of the Pallium and Conferral of the Fisherman's Ring for the Beginning of the Petrine Ministry of the Bishop of Rome", April 24, 2005, https://w2.vatican.va/content/benedict-xvi/en/homilies/2005/documents /hf_ben-xvi_hom_20050424_inizio-pontificato.html.

The Catholic view is now, as it has been from the beginning, that the pope has primacy of authority and jurisdiction. But John Paul II, speaking to Eastern concerns, has
said that while the pope's authority to rule is granted by
Christ to Peter, how that primacy is actually exercised is
open to discussion.[5]

It's important to remember the collegial aspect of the
Church. Every bishop in the world is somehow responsible for the Church as a whole, not just his own diocese,
and he works with the pope in exercising that responsibility, as in the following.

- *Meetings among bishops.* These go by a variety of
  names—consistories, synods, and councils. They all
  bring bishops and the pope together to further the
  work of the Church. An ecumenical council is a
  meeting of all the world's bishops. To be binding, the
  decisions of an ecumenical council must be approved
  by the pope.
- *Meetings of bishops with the pope.* Each bishop travels
  every five years to Rome for a visit *ad limina apostolorum* (to the "threshold of the apostles"). A twelve-
  hundred-year-old custom, this visit is a time for a
  bishop to report to the pope on his diocese and to
  receive the pope's guidance.
- *Meetings among administrative bodies.* As the Church
  grew in size and complexity, the pope created agencies of bishops, priests, and deacons to help him
  administer it. Together, these agencies make up
  the Roman Curia. (Each diocese has a similar, but
  smaller, body to assist the bishop.) The Curia includes
  the *Secretariat of State* that relates to governments and

[5] John Paul II, *Ut Unum Sint*, no. 95.

other international organizations (e.g., the United Nations), *congregations* that govern various aspects of Church life (such as doctrine, worship, and so on), *councils* for promoting various Church activities like dialogue with other religions, and *tribunals* for judging disputes. These groups all report to the pope.

- *Meetings of cardinals with the pope.* The pope has specially designated men—cardinals—who are among his key advisors. The title *cardinal* comes from the Latin word for "hinge" (*cardo*), signifying the important role that cardinals play in the Church. Metaphorically, they are the hinges on which the administration of the Church turns. The pope can appoint a deacon or a priest to be a cardinal, though in recent times almost all cardinals are bishops. The College of Cardinals is responsible for electing the next pope.

Popes see their role in the Church as one of service. Jesus taught that authority meant service, not domination (Mk 10:43–45; Jn 13:14–15). Peter warns other Church leaders not to be domineering over those in their charge (1 Pet 5:1–3). Modern popes take this lesson seriously. In 1975, Paul VI stressed that "our authority is ordained to service",[6] a theme echoed by John Paul II and Benedict XVI, and dear to the heart of Pope Francis.

Among the pope's titles is *Servus Servorum Dei* (Servant of the Servants of God). Pope Saint Gregory I (590–604) originated the title and applied it to himself. It was his favorite, because for him it captured the heart of the papacy. When the pope is referred to by several of his

---

[6] Paul VI, Lenten discourse to the Roman clergy, February 10, 1975, in *L'Osservatore Romano* 8 (February 10, 1975), p. 3.

titles, this title is usually mentioned last. It best expresses the spirit in which he uses his authority.

The Pope as Reconciler

Heresies cause great damage to individuals and churches, yet the Holy Spirit can use heresies to lead the Church into a deeper understanding of her faith. It was often the appearance of heresy that forced the Church to defend and define the true doctrine. The popes faithfully walked the fine line of orthodoxy and carefully and precisely taught and defined the Catholic faith.

From the earliest years a bewildering variety of false teachings rose up against the Catholic faith. Some of these false teachings took their names from the doctrine they taught (such as Monophysitism, the belief that Jesus had only one nature). Others were named after the men who started the heresy (such as Arianism, from Arius, who taught that Jesus was simply a created demigod). Some heresies, like Nestorianism, began as an unfortunate misunderstanding of the faith. Others like Manichaeism (which denied the goodness of matter) were really separate religions that wanted to use Christian terminology.

Modern Catholics often don't understand why heresies are so serious. Heresy is a twisting of truth and leads not only to false beliefs but to practices that jeopardize salvation. Heresy is like crab grass—you can pull out clumps of it, but the roots send out runners to other parts of the lawn. They have a tendency to recur in different forms in different eras of Christian history. Certain ideas that were common among the Gnostic heretics in the second and third centuries reappeared in Manichaeism in the fifth century, in Albigensianism in the tenth, and again in the New Age movement today.

Throughout Church history, individual theologians, bishops, and councils struggled to eradicate heresy and to protect the Catholic faithful from its effects. In the process, they helped clarify the truth. But the efforts of local bishops had limited scope. A local bishop might remove someone like Arius from his church, but Arius would simply take his heresy elsewhere and gain additional followers. Only someone in a position of *universal* authority could deal with the situation for *all* the churches.

Popes responded by defending the truth, protecting the faithful, and reconciling the heretics whenever possible.

To deal with various heresies, Rome would consult with bishops and either publish a doctrinal clarification or instruct a local council on how to proceed. Asked how the bishop of Alexandria should have dealt with the Sabellian heresy (which held that the Trinity is one divine Person with different manifestations), Pope Saint Dionysius (259–268) called a synod of bishops and wrote a letter explaining Catholic teaching on the Trinity— almost a century before the doctrine was formally defined at Nicaea in 325.

The goal of Rome's efforts in such matters is to protect the faithful from the plague of false teaching. This means making sure the truth is proclaimed effectively and removing the cause of the confusion. Sometimes the pope could persuade a heretic to return to the truth. If not, he disciplined the heretic, including even excommunicating him, to bring the offender to his senses. But excommunication is strong medicine, so popes do not use it lightly.

Rome also strives to reconcile the offender and his followers. Part of the apostolic ministry is reconciling sinners to God (2 Cor 5:18–20).[7] But reconciliation can be a slow process; sometimes it takes centuries.

---

[7] See John Paul II, *Ut Unum Sint*, no. 99.

The pressure for Church reform, building through-out the fifteenth century, finally exploded early in the sixteenth. But even as Protestantism pursued reform by breaking with the Church, several reform movements were under way within the Church. With papal approval, six new religious orders appeared, including the Jesuits, the Capuchin friars (a Franciscan reform), and the Ursulines. Still, the situation demanded more direct papal action.

The Protestant Reformers challenged Church author-ity, theology, sacramental life, and morality. At first slow to respond, the papacy called for a council to defend Cath-olic doctrine and institute reforms. The Council of Trent continued through the reign of three popes—Paul III (1534–1549), Julius III (1550–1555), and Pius IV (1559–1565). The popes even invited Protestants to attend, but they refused.

Despite its thorough labor, Trent might have ended as a dead letter had not the next four popes dedicated themselves to carrying out its reforms. They published a Churchwide catechism known as the *Roman Catechism* or the *Catechism of the Council of Trent* (which is still in print and which served as a model for today's *Catechism of the Catholic Church*), stan-dardized the Mass and the Divine Office (now called Lit-urgy of the Hours), founded seminaries to educate clergy, reformed the Curia, and created a system of papal delega-tions to all corners of a rapidly expanding world (see One-ness of Faith on p. 35).

Yet, reconciliation with Protestants is glacially slow. Efforts toward unity remained somewhat a grassroots effort within Catholicism until Pope John XXIII sum-moned the Second Vatican Council in 1959, and invited Christians of other traditions to attend. This time, some did. In the documents on the Church (*Lumen Gentium*) and on restoring unity (*Unitatis Redintegratio*), the council

Catechism of the Council of Trent on Oneness of Faith

"Should anyone object that the Church is content with one Head and one Spouse, Jesus Christ, and requires no other, the answer is obvious. For as we deem Christ not only the author of all the sacraments, but also their invisible minister—He it is who baptizes, He it is who absolves, although men are appointed by Him the external ministers of the sacraments—so has He placed over His Church, which He governs by His invisible Spirit, a man to be His vicar and the minister of His power.

"A visible Church requires a visible head; therefore the Savior appointed Peter head and pastor of all the faithful, when he committed to his care the feeding of all His sheep, in such ample terms that he willed the very same power of ruling and governing the entire Church to descend on Peter's successors." (*Catechism of the Council of Trent*, 2nd rev. ed., trans. J. A. McHugh and C. J. Cullan [Rockford, Ill.: TAN Books and Publishers, 1982], p. 104)

clarified membership in the Church, the relationship of the Catholic Church to non-Catholic Christians, and the Catholic understanding of ecumenism.

Efforts to reconcile with the Eastern Orthodox have also moved slowly. There are indications now that we gradually may be nearing some form of reconciliation. The Second Vatican Council strengthened the Eastern Catholic ritual churches and hoped that those churches would help reunite Catholics with their Orthodox brothers. While the council was meeting in Rome, Paul VI flew to Jerusalem to reopen paths of communication with Patriarch Athenagoras of Constantinople. There, both sides lifted the excommunications leveled by their predecessors in 1054.

Since then, the pace of contact and dialogue has quickened. Particularly important was the 1994 Common Christological Declaration signed by Pope John Paul II and Mar Dinkha IV, Catholicos-Patriarch of the Assyrian Church of the East. This joint declaration states the churches' common belief in the human and divine natures of the one Person of Jesus Christ—a declaration that clears up a fifteen-hundred-year-old misunderstanding.

Pope John Paul II's 1995 apostolic letter *Orientale Lumen* (The Light of the East) aims to "safeguard the significance of the Eastern traditions for the whole church" and to aid the restoration of unity.[8] The pope's ardent wish for reunification led him and his successors to increase the number of contacts with leaders from as many Orthodox churches as possible.

Now that it has a renewed vision for ecumenical action, the Church is committed to pursuing it. Pope Paul VI established what is now the Pontifical Council for Promoting Christian Unity. He also began a process of theological dialogue, which has borne significant fruit.

John Paul II acknowledged that his office requires the pope to pursue unity (see Role of Papacy on p. 37). His 1995 encyclical letter *Ut Unum Sint* (That They May Be One) reminds Catholics that unity "is not a matter of adding together all the riches scattered throughout the various

---

[8] John Paul II, *Orientale Lumen* (May 2, 1995), no. 1, http://w2.vatican.va /content/john-paul-ii/en/apost_letters/1995/documents/hf_jp-ii_apl _19950502_orientale-lumen.html.

Role of Papacy in the Work of Unity

"When the Catholic Church affirms that the office of the Bishop of Rome corresponds to the will of Christ, she does not separate this office from the mission entrusted to the whole body of Bishops, who are also 'vicars and ambassadors of Christ' (*Lumen Gentium* 27). The Bishop of Rome is a member of the 'college', and the Bishops are his brothers in the ministry.

"Whatever relates to the unity of all Christian communities clearly forms part of the concerns of the primacy. As Bishop of Rome I am fully aware ... that Christ ardently desires the full and visible communion of all those Communities in which, by virtue of God's faithfulness, his Spirit dwells.

"I am convinced that I have a particular responsibility in this regard, above all in acknowledging the ecumenical aspirations of the majority of the Christian Communities and in heeding the request made of me to find a way of exercising the primacy which, while in no way renouncing what is essential to its mission, is nonetheless open to a new situation. For a whole millennium Christians were united in 'a brotherly fraternal communion of faith and sacramental life.... If disagreements in belief and discipline arose among them, the Roman See acted by common consent as moderator' (*Unitatis Redintegratio* 14).

"In this way the primacy exercised its office of unity." (John Paul II, *Ut Unum Sint*, no. 95)

Christian Communities in order to arrive at a Church which God has in mind for the future",[9] much less of denying any truth just to make people feel good about one another. Who would respect such a false unity? Rather, "elements of this already-given Church exist, found in their fullness in the Catholic Church and, without this fullness, in the other Communities, where certain features of the Christian mystery have at times been more effectively emphasized".[10]

The Pope as Evangelist

In 1949, Father Leonard Feeney, an American college chaplain, caused an uproar by claiming that Protestants could not be saved. They were outside the Catholic Church, he said, and "outside the Church there is no salvation."[11] Father Feeney was quoting Saint Cyprian of Carthage (d. 258)[12] but misapplying his dictum. Told by the Vatican to desist, Feeney refused and was excommunicated after he accused the archbishop of Boston of teaching heresy by acknowledging that non-Catholics could be saved. (Fortunately, Feeney was reconciled before his death.)

So, what *does* "outside the Church there is no salvation" mean? The *Catechism* replies: "Re-formulated positively, it means that all salvation comes from Christ the Head through the Church which is his Body" (*CCC* 846). The sign and means of salvation is baptism; and valid baptism

[9] John Paul II, *Ut Unum Sint*, no. 14.

[10] Ibid.

[11] Michael J. Feldberg, S.J., "American Heretic: The Rise and Fall of Father Leonard Feeney", *American Catholic Studies* 123, no. 2 (Summer 2012): 109–15, https://muse.jhu.edu/article/483741/pdf.

[12] Cyprian, Epistle 73, 21, quoted by John Paul II, "All Salvation Comes through Christ", General Audience (May 31, 1995), *L'Osservatore Romano* (June 7, 1995), p. 11.

brings one into a definite (if sometimes partial) communion with the Catholic Church. Quoting *Lumen Gentium*, the *Catechism* further states that the affirmation that salvation is found only in the Catholic Church is not directed to those who through no fault of their own are baptized in other Christian communions but to those who, "knowing that the Catholic Church was founded as necessary by God through Christ, would refuse either to enter it or to remain in it" (*LG* 14) (see Fourth Lateran Ecumenical Council on p. 40).

One of the most ancient of the pope's titles is *Pontifex Maximus*, usually translated "Supreme Pontiff". A *pontiff* is a builder of bridges. The title originally belonged to the Roman emperors, who saw themselves as the bridge between their subjects and the gods. In 375, Emperor Gratian rejected the title for himself and applied it to Pope Saint Damasus I, who served the *true* God. The pope thought the title fitting because of his evangelistic role. If, as Pope Paul VI taught in *Evangelii Nuntiandi* (Proclaiming the Gospel), the Church "exists in order to evangelize",[13] then the pope is her foremost evangelist. He must take the lead in bridging the gap between unbelievers and Christ by bringing them into the Mystical Body of Christ, the Church.

Evangelization begins by being evangelized. People don't evangelize themselves; they come to faith in the gospel by hearing it from others (Rom 10:17). Only when one is converted himself can he effectively evangelize others. For this reason, the pope spends much of his time preaching and teaching (a topic the next chapter will take up in more detail).

[13] Paul VI, *Evangelii Nuntiandi* (December 8, 1975), no. 14, http://w2 .vatican.va/content/paul-vi/en/apost_exhortations/documents/hf_p-vi_exh _19751208_evangelii-nuntiandi.html.

Fourth Lateran Ecumenical Council on the Need for Communion with the Church

"One indeed is the universal Church of the faithful, outside which no one at all is saved, in which the priest himself is the sacrifice, Jesus Christ, whose body and blood are truly contained in the sacrament of the altar under the species of bread and wine; the bread [changed] into His body by the divine power of transubstantiation, and the wine into the blood, so that to accomplish the mystery of unity we ourselves receive from His [nature] what He Himself received from ours.

"And surely no one can accomplish this sacrament except a priest who has been rightly ordained according to the keys of the Church which Jesus Christ Himself conceded to the apostles and to their successors.

"But the sacrament of baptism (which at the invocation of God and the indivisible Trinity, namely, of the Father and of the Son and of the Holy Spirit, is solemnized in water) rightly conferred by anyone in the form of the Church is useful unto salvation for little ones and for adults.

"And if, after the reception of baptism, anyone shall have lapsed into sin, through true penance he can always be restored. Moreover, not only virgins and the continent but also married persons pleasing to God through right faith and good work merit to arrive at a blessed eternity." (Fourth Lateran Council [1215], canon 1, translation from *Decrees of the Ecumenical Councils*, ed. Norman P. Tanner [Washington, D.C.: Georgetown University Press, 1990])

The first bishop of Rome, Saint Peter, is known to have traveled the Roman Empire, preaching Jesus Christ. After spreading the gospel in Judea and Samaria, Peter took it to the world. Dionysius of Corinth (c. 170) wrote that Peter had "planted" the church in Corinth along with Paul.[14] In his *History of the Church*, Eusebius (c. 260-c. 340) describes Peter as an evangelist preaching throughout much of Asia Minor,[15] and Saint John Chrysostom refers to Peter as the "teacher of the world".[16]

The popes of the early Church laid down their lives evangelizing the world and building up the Church. As martyrs, they gave witness to the faith. Indeed, the word *martyr* comes from the Greek word for witness (*martus*). This was the ultimate evangelism and, as Tertullian wrote, "The blood of the martyrs is the seed of Christians."[17]

From the very beginning, the popes have always taken a keen interest in missionary activity, sending missionaries to areas of greatest need and supporting the churches founded there. In 596, Pope Saint Gregory I sent Augustine of Canterbury with forty monks to evangelize England. In 719, Pope Saint Gregory II sent Boniface to Germany. During the period of global exploration in the sixteenth and seventeenth centuries, the popes sent Jesuit and Franciscan

[14] "The Letter of Dionysius of Corinth to Soger of Rome", quoted in Eusebius, *History of the Church* 2.25.8, http://www.documentacatholicaomnia .eu/03d/0265-0339,_Eusebius_Caesariensis,_Church_History,_EN.pdf.

[15] Eusebius, *History of the Church* 3.4.2.

[16] John Chrysostom, *Homilies on the Gospel of St. John*, homily 88, in *A Library of Fathers of the Holy Catholic Church: Anterior to the Division of the East and the West* (Oxford: John Henry Parker; London: F. and J. Rivington, 1853), p. 793.

[17] Tertullian, "The Apology", in *Latin Christianity: Its Founder, Tertullian*, ed. Alexander Roberts, James Donaldson, and A. Cleveland Coxe, trans. S. Thelwall, vol. 3 of The Ante-Nicene Fathers (Buffalo, N.Y.: Christian Literature Company, 1885), p. 55.

missionaries to Africa, Asia, and the Americas to evangelize the natives there. A multitude of missionary orders
sprang up. Several popes, starting with Pope Saint Pius V,
worked to centralize missionary efforts; but not until the
founding of the Congregation for the Propagation of
the Faith in 1622 did a stable coordinating body emerge.

To encourage evangelism among non-Christians, the
pope is also interested in building bridges between Christians and members of non-Christian religions, particularly
Judaism and Islam. In both cases, there is much ground to
cover but work proceeds in earnest.

Christians have not always remembered that their religion originates in and is the fulfillment of Judaism. The
Catholic Church is like a flower that blossomed from the
Jewish root. Any serious study of the New Testament will
reveal the Jewishness of Jesus, as well as that of his mother
and foster father, all of the apostles, and most early Christians. Catholicism incorporates many Judaic elements in
both its doctrines and its liturgy. Unfortunately, a variety
of historical factors led some Christians to accuse Jews of
deicide ("murder of God"), and to marginalize them polit-
ically and socially.

The horror of the Holocaust helped to change all that.
Popes Pius XI and Pius XII protested Nazi repression of
Jews, but the Nazis in response stepped up their depor-
tations and mass killings. Jewish leaders themselves asked
Pius XII not to protest too loudly, because each time he
did their situation became worse. But if the pope had to
keep a low profile, he still could work in other ways. He
hid many thousands of Jews in Vatican City and at his own
summer residence, ordered religious buildings in Rome
to open themselves as places of refuge, and provided large
sums of money in aid. After the war, it became apparent
that Pius XII was responsible for saving more Jewish lives

than all of the secular relief organizations combined. The smear campaign against Pius XII that started in the 1960s and continues to this day has no basis in fact and has been refuted time and again.

Because of the war experience, the time was right for changes in the relationship between the two communities. The Second Vatican Council document *Nostra Aetate* repudiated the charge of deicide and denounced anti-Semitism in any form.[18] In 1974, Paul VI established the Commission for Religious Relations with the Jews. John Paul II went even further, recognizing the State of Israel, publicly deploring past Catholic offenses against Jews, and taking part in numerous Holocaust memorials both in Poland (the location of Auschwitz) and in Jerusalem. Each subsequent papacy has nourished these relationships through both words and deeds.

Nostra Aetate, the same Vatican II document that addressed relations with Jews, also touched on relations with Muslims. It pleaded with both sides to promote "social justice and moral welfare, as well as peace and freedom".[19] While relationships between the two religions are strained in many ways, recent popes have been reaching out in meetings with Muslim leaders and delegations, both in Rome and on trips abroad.

The first pope poured out his blood to spread the good news of Jesus Christ, and his successors have carried on the same work. Peter reminded the Church, "With the Lord one day is as a thousand years, and a thousand years as one day" (2 Pet 3:8). So it is with the work of

---

[18] Vatican Council II, Declaration on the Relation of the Church to Non-Christian Religions *Nostra Aetate* (October 28, 1965), http://www.vatican.va /archive/hist_councils/ii_vatican_council/documents/vat-ii_decl_19651028 _nostra-aetate_en.html.

[19] Ibid., no. 3.

evangelization, reconciliation, and reunification. When all of these are done in the Holy Spirit, the work of God *will* be accomplished.

The Pope as Global Shepherd

In *Ut Unum Sint*, Pope John Paul II distinguished between the office of the papacy and the way that office is exercised.[20] The former is a permanent feature of the Church; Peter will always have a successor with full teaching, governing, and sanctifying authority. The latter changes all the time in both small and large ways. Two changes are especially noteworthy both for how they shape the pope's ministry and for what they portend for the future: papal travels and the "globalization" of the cardinals who elect the pope.

For most of papal history, the pope stayed rather close to the city of Rome but would take relatively short trips as need arose, mainly within Italy and southern Europe. Because of political changes in Italy during the nineteenth century, popes from Blessed Pius IX (1846–1878) through Pius XI (1922–1939) confined themselves to the palace of the Vatican. Political tensions eased in 1929 when the Lateran Treaty created Vatican City as an independent state with the pope as its head; but even so, Pius XI remained within Vatican confines. His successor Pius XII continued the practice. That began to change with the accession of Pope John XXIII, who surprised everyone by leaving the Vatican for impromptu visits to hospitals and prisons around Rome. Paul VI set the current trend by traveling abroad to six continents, most famously meeting with Orthodox Patriarch Athenagoras I in Jerusalem in 1964.

[20]John Paul II, *Ut Unum Sint*, no. 96.

Subsequent popes have traveled widely around the globe, bringing the gospel to every land, personally encouraging the faithful everywhere, and strengthening or establishing ties with various Christian and non-Christian groups. As long as circumstances allow, papal journeys abroad will form a vital part of the pope's apostolic ministry.

Another change is the international character of the College of Cardinals. Because the pope is the bishop of the Diocese of Rome, the College of Cardinals was originally created to assist him as members of what is called the "papal household" in his relationships with other bishops and civil leaders. As the Church expanded, the "household" became larger. The pope assigned cardinals to represent him in various countries and to advise him on developments within the Church there. They also took on the responsibility of electing the next pope, usually from among their own number.

Cardinals have always come from various countries, mostly representing the northern hemisphere, especially Europe. But recent popes have been responding to the explosive growth of the Church in Asia, Africa, and South America by appointing cardinals from those cultures. Often, those cardinals serve in areas of the Church that are suffering oppression, are poor and historically marginalized, or are coping with difficulties that affect the Church as a whole. In addition, the pope is adding to the College of Cardinals bishops from Eastern churches in union with Rome. What do these changes mean for the papacy?

They mean changes in how the Church sees herself, as represented by the type of bishop the cardinals will select to become a future pope. A more international College of Cardinals means first that the focus of attention in the Church is shifting from Europe and the northern hemisphere to the East and the South. Second, the cardinals with the most influence are less likely to be those from wealthy and important archdioceses, and more likely to be from remote but growing geographical areas. Third, the Eastern Catholic churches are coming into greater prominence, highlighting that the Catholic Church embraces more than just the Latin Church.

Jesus commanded his apostles to go into the whole world, baptizing them and teaching them to observe all that he commanded (Mt 28:20). They have obeyed, and today's Church is growing in new and exciting places. Without ceasing to be the bishop of Rome, the pope who leads and shepherds a worldwide Church may in the future come from one of these nontraditional areas, as the current pope has.

Chapter 3

The Pope as Teacher

All popes teach. Some come to their office with a suitcase crammed with credentials. Others arrive more lightly packed. But whether equipped for it or not, all popes are teachers by virtue of their office. Teaching—part of what Jesus called "feeding [his] sheep" (Jn 21:17)—is one of the pope's main responsibilities.

This chapter discusses what the pope teaches about, how he teaches it, what it means for him to teach infallibly, why the pope teaches, and why it matters to you.

What the Pope Teaches About

When Jesus stood up to speak, he usually surprised his audience (see Jn 6; Mt 5–7). Jesus' unique teaching cost him disciples and eventually his life. Popes who are his vicars must expect that their teachings also will be countercultural—*and* potentially have a similar outcome.

Two cases in point, one ancient and one modern: Peter told Jesus he was willing to lay down his life for him (Mt 26:35). And during his lifetime Peter spoke the truth even though his own people opposed him and Roman soldiers arrested and imprisoned him (e.g., Acts 12:1–5). After a lifetime of serving his risen Lord, Peter was crucified for the Catholic faith, head downward, in Nero's Circus in Rome.

A modern example of popes standing against their culture took place just after the Second Vatican Council. Many Catholics thought that Pope Paul VI could relax the age-old ban on contraception and endorse the use of the birth-control pill. Fully aware of the implications, Pope Paul took a long time to study and pray. Then in July 1968, he published *Humanae Vitae*, which confirmed the traditional teaching (see Paul VI on p. 49). His encyclical met with protests so fierce that the tidal wave of dissent is still felt today. Despite the clash with the modern culture, the pope faithfully held to the revealed truth of Christian teaching.

Authoritative papal teaching is principally concerned with faith and morals. It can also touch on certain other matters needed to safeguard or elaborate points of faith and morals. It is based on the word of God as contained in Scripture and Tradition and in God's self-disclosure through the created world.

In the first chapter of Romans, Paul argues that "what can be known about God is plain to them, because God has shown it to them" (1:19). Creation reveals truth about God: "his invisible nature, namely, his eternal power and deity, has been clearly perceived in the things that have been made" (1:20). Paul also argues that this knowledge should lead men to seek a right relationship with God (1:18–21).

So it's important that we understand who God is, because we are destined to spend eternity with him. Truth is perceived through the mind and the will, through what we know through reason and faith and how we respond by choice. The whole New Testament is full of warnings that proper faith and morals have to be explained, guarded, and insisted on. It is about these two matters that the pope

Paul VI Teaching on the Regulation of Births

"In conformity with these landmarks in the human and Christian vision of marriage, we must once again declare that the direct interruption of the generative process already begun, and, above all, directly willed and procured abortion, even if for therapeutic reasons, are to be absolutely excluded as licit means of regulating birth.

"Equally to be condemned, as the magisterium of the Church has affirmed on many occasions, is direct sterilization, whether of the man or of the woman, whether perpetual or temporary. Similarly excluded is any action which either before, at the moment of, or after sexual intercourse, is specifically intended to prevent procreation— whether as an end or as a means." (Paul VI, Encyclical Letter on the Regulation of Birth *Humanae Vitae* [July 25, 1968], no. 14)

has a primary duty and right to teach, in order to safeguard the truths of faith and morals. He also has occasion to touch on other matters, such as natural law.

Natural law is the ability of man to recognize through rational reflection how he ought to act. The words *ought to* are important. They imply a moral element. A psychologist studying the behavior of squirrels can speak of "normal squirrel behavior", like collecting nuts. But the psychologist would not say that the squirrel "ought to" collect nuts, or that it "ought not" refuse to collect them. Such statements would imply that the squirrel has a moral sense.

The study of human behavior, on the other hand, reveals an awareness of circumstances (in common with squirrels), and that certain responses to them can be "right" or "wrong" (a judgment squirrels can't make). Human actions occur within a framework of right versus wrong. Men can even choose to do things they know are wrong. It doesn't take religion, says Saint Paul, to make that clear, since there is a "law" written on the heart, where the "conscience also bears witness and ... conflicting thoughts accuse or perhaps excuse" (Rom 2:15).

Papal teaching based on natural law means that the pope is explaining the moral truth of things individuals can and should recognize. The moral principles expressed in the Ten Commandments fall into this category.

But not everything we need to know about either God or how we should act comes from natural law. There are certain things about God that he has to tell us before we can know them—for example, that God is a Trinity of Persons. This truth is not obvious to our human senses. We learn these things through revelation, God's disclosure to mankind.

Scripture is a written form of revelation. It "must be acknowledged as teaching solidly, faithfully and without error that truth which God wanted put into sacred writings, for the sake of salvation."[1] Scripture addresses both faith (e.g., God is One and is a Person) and morality (e.g., that we should love God). "All Scripture is inspired by God and profitable for teaching, for reproof, for correction, and for training in righteousness" (2 Tim 3:16). Being inspired ("God breathed") does not therefore mean

---

[1] Vatican Council II, Dogmatic Constitution on Divine Revelation *Dei Verbum* (November 18, 1965), no. 11, http://www.vatican.va/archive/hist _councils/ii_vatican_council/documents/vat-ii_const_19651118_dei-verbum _en.html.

that it contains exhaustive truth. Scripture leaves out a lot of things (e.g., see Jn 20:30–31; 21:25), and sometimes Tradition is required to understand the teaching of Scripture properly. Papal teaching draws on both Scripture and Tradition.

Tradition is handing down the Christian faith intact from one generation to the next. The Church must keep her teaching free from dilution and error. Paul warns his disciple Timothy to guard carefully what he has received (1 Tim 6:20), to preach Christian truth in its integrity (1 Tim 4:6–16), and to do so fearlessly (2 Tim 1:7). Timothy must appoint others who can teach when he is gone (2 Tim 2:1–2). These Scripture passages point to a teaching role or office—*magisterium* in Latin—which the apostles passed on to their successors, the bishops. The Magisterium is exercised by the pope and the bishops in union with him. Other teachers, like theologians and catechists, may be delegated by the bishops to instruct the faithful, but they are not part of the Magisterium. Even most Doctors of the Church, who helped the Church understand the deposit of faith, didn't belong to the Magisterium, because most of them were not bishops.

How the Pope Teaches

The pope recognizes his need for the assistance of the Holy Spirit when he teaches. He spends a lot of time in prayer concerning his teaching. Some popes, as John Paul II was, are in the habit of writing while sitting or kneeling before the Blessed Sacrament.

The pope today is constantly teaching. On trips, at home, during liturgies, at meetings of bishops, or in audiences, he delivers hundreds of messages every year. He must adapt his messages to different circumstances, and the forms he uses evolve over time. One pope develops a format that proves useful, a later pope refines it, and eventually it becomes standard form.

It is convenient to divide papal teachings into those delivered "live" (orally) and those meant for written distribution. In each category are forms that have different degrees of gravity.

Oral teaching includes informal remarks, homilies, daily Angelus messages, and audience addresses. Though these are among the papal utterances that have the least gravity, they can on occasion contain material that will come to have great prominence. Pope John Paul II began the custom of using the Wednesday General Audiences to provide extended catecheses on important topics. In a series of audiences delivered over a period of five years, he explored his "theology of the body", which is now a staple of many theology programs around the world. Subsequent popes have taken up the practice of providing extended instruction through these General Audiences.

Written teachings include encyclicals and other letters, bulls, apostolic constitutions, and apostolic exhortations— among others.

Much of the New Testament consists of "circular letters", or *encyclicals*, written to be read in all the churches (cf. Col 4:16). Peter's first epistle was sent to a wide range of churches in Asia Minor (cf. 1 Pet 1:1); but it, like his second epistle, differs from any modern papal document in that Peter's are divinely inspired.

The modern practice of popes writing encyclicals began with Pope Benedict XIV (1740–1758). Modern encyclicals tend to discuss one topic in depth. They may deal with different kinds of doctrinal questions, such as John Paul II's gospel teaching on the dignity of human life (*Evangelium Vitae*, 1995) (see Pope John Paul II on p. 53), or issues of

social morality, like Leo XIII's encyclical about the rights
of workers (*Rerum Novarum*, 1891) (see Pope Leo XIII on
p. 54), or Gregory XVI's apostolic letter on the evils of
chattel slavery (*In Supremo*, 1839) (see Pope Gregory XVI
on p. 55).

Some develop spiritual themes, such as John Paul II's
encyclical about the role of Mary in the life of a Christian

Pope John Paul II on the Dignity of Human Life

"Man is called to a fullness of life which far
exceeds the dimensions of his earthly existence,
because it consists in sharing the very life of God.
The loftiness of this supernatural vocation reveals
the greatness and the inestimable value of human
life even in its temporal phase. Life in time, in
fact, is the fundamental condition, the initial stage
and an integral part of the entire unified process
of human existence. It is a process which, unex-
pectedly and undeservedly, is enlightened by the
promise and renewed by the gift of divine life,
which will reach its full realization in eternity (cf.
1 Jn 3:1–2). At the same time, it is precisely this
supernatural calling which highlights the relative
character of each individual's earthly life. After
all, life on earth is not an 'ultimate' but a 'penul-
timate' reality; even so, it remains a sacred reality
entrusted to us, to be preserved with a sense of
responsibility and brought to perfection in love
and in the gift of ourselves to God and to our
brothers and sisters." (John Paul II, Encyclical
Letter on the Gospel of Life *Evangelium Vitae*
[March 28, 1995], no. 2)

Pope Leo XIII on the Rights of Workers

"If citizens have free right to associate, as in fact they do, they also must have the right freely to adopt the organization and the rules which they judge most appropriate to achieve their purpose [of being paid a just wage and maintaining humane working conditions].... In summary, let this be laid down as a general and constant law: Workers' associations ought to be so constituted and so governed as to furnish the most suitable and most convenient means to attain the object proposed, which consists in this, that the individual members of the association secure, so far as possible, an increase in the goods of body, of soul, and of prosperity." (Leo XIII, Encyclical Letter on the Condition of the Working Classes [*Rerum Novarum*], May 15, 1891, no. 76 [Boston, Mass.: St. Paul, 1942])

(*Redemptoris Mater*, 1987). While most encyclicals are addressed to bishops, some are addressed to others, including lay Catholics, non-Catholic Christians, and even "all men of good will". For example, John XXIII addressed his encyclical on world peace (*Pacem in Terris*, 1963) to several groups including, finally, "all men of good will" (see Pope John XXIII on p. 56). The record holder for the number of encyclicals written is Pope Leo XIII, who wrote seventy-five, roughly three a year.

Important as encyclicals are, other types of documents can be actually more important in terms of their solemnity or authority.

Pope Gregory XVI Condemns Slavery of Blacks and Indians

"The slave trade, although it has diminished, is still carried on by numerous Christians. Therefore, desiring to remove such a shame from all the Christian peoples and walking in the footsteps of Our Predecessors, We, by apostolic authority, warn and strongly exhort in the Lord faithful Christians of every condition that no one in the future dare to bother unjustly, despoil of their possessions, or reduce to Slavery, Indians, Blacks or other such peoples. Nor are they to lend aid and favor to those who give themselves up to these practices, or exercise that inhuman traffic by which the Blacks, as if they were not humans but rather animals, having been brought into slavery in no matter what way, are, without any distinction and contrary to the rights of justice and humanity, bought, sold, and sometimes given over to the hardest labor." (Pope Gregory XVI, *In Supremo* [December 3, 1839], in Joel S. Panzer, "The Popes and Slavery: Setting the Record Straight", quoted in *The Catholic Answer*, January/February 1996 [Huntington, Ind.: Our Sunday Visitor])

If you've read much European history, you've doubtless run across references to a *papal bull*. This type of document doesn't refer to an animal. Rather, the name comes from the Latin word *bulla*, meaning a confidential seal. The seal was made of lead or wax and was used to ensure that the document was authentic. The bull was often used for communications of major importance, including appointments

Pope John XXIII on the Nuclear Arms Race

"We are deeply distressed to see the enormous stocks of armaments that have been, and continue to be, manufactured in the economically more developed countries. This policy is involving a vast outlay of intellectual and material resources....

"Justice,... right reason, and the recognition of man's dignity cry out insistently for a cessation of the arms race. The stock-piles of armaments which have been built up in various countries must be reduced all round and simultaneously by the parties concerned. Nuclear weapons must be banned. A general agreement must be reached on a suitable disarmament program, with an effective system of mutual control." (John XXIII, *Pacem in Terris* [April 11, 1963], nos. 109, 112, http://w2.vatican.va/content/john-xxiii/en /encyclicals/documents/hf_j-xxiii_enc_11041963 _pacem.html)

of bishops or canonizations. Though not usually a teaching document, it can be used to make an infallible pronouncement, as was Pius XII's definition of Mary's Assumption into heaven in the 1950 bull *Munificentissimus Deus*.

Another document of high authority is the *apostolic constitution*. It deals with major doctrinal, disciplinary, or administrative matters. For example, the *Catechism of the Catholic Church* summarizes basic Church teachings, so the pope prefaced it with an apostolic constitution on the deposit of faith by John Paul II (*Fidei Depositum*, 1992).

An *apostolic exhortation* is a papal document written to encourage individuals dealing with a particular effort or situation; an exhortation often appears in conjunction with the conclusion of episcopal synods. It presents the papal viewpoint, usually by underscoring the synod's importance and encouraging the bishops to implement their decisions. For example, the newly elected John Paul II wrote the 1979 *Catechesi Tradendae* in response to the 1977 Synod of Bishops on catechesis, which defines what catechesis is and how it should be delivered.

A less formal document is a *letter* that the pope may write to worldwide audiences on different topics, such as John Paul II's *Letter to Families* (1994), his insight on the dignity and role of women (*Mulieris Dignitatem*, 1988), or preparations for the Great Jubilee (*Tertio Millennio Adveniente*, 1994) and its sequel (*Novo Millennio Ineunte*, 2001).

The Church's "ordinary Magisterium" conveys most of the Church's teaching, whether that teaching is by the pope or the bishops teaching in union with him. On rare occasions, the pope may need to present a teaching infallibly. And that gets us into the Church's "extraordinary Magisterium".

What It Means When the Pope Teaches Infallibly

Earlier, we learned that Jesus gave Peter a position of authority, by giving him "the keys of the kingdom of heaven" with authority to "bind" and "loose" (Mt 16:19). What Peter declared on earth, God would ratify in heaven! This meant that God would have to superintend or oversee Peter's words to prevent him from binding others to believe something false. We also learned that Jesus charged Peter to strengthen his fellow apostles in their faith (Lk 22:32) and to "feed [his] sheep" (Jn 21:17)—both of which involve a teaching role. But Jesus said more.

After the Last Supper, Jesus promised the Twelve that he would send the Holy Spirit to lead them into the truth (Jn 16:13). The Spirit would reveal things to them about sin, righteousness, and judgment (Jn 16:8–11). Further, that revelation would come from the Father; and it would unfold in its fullness over time. Jesus taught the truth because he *is* the truth (Jn 14:6). Likewise, his apostles would witness to the truth (Mt 28:19–20).

Because the Holy Spirit, not mere human insight, would lead the apostles (Jn 16:13–15), Jesus commissioned them to speak for God. In response the people were required to listen with all attentiveness and obedience. Though new public revelation ended with the death of the last apostle (cf. *CCC* 66), and the Magisterium of the Church is not divinely inspired as is Sacred Scripture, the Church is nevertheless protected by the charism of infallibility, making her "the pillar and bulwark of the truth" (1 Tim 3:15; cf. *CCC* 171). Because infallibility as a charism of the Holy Spirit protects the Church from teaching error, it follows that the pope cannot teach "infallibly" anything contrary to the truths of the faith.

Infallibility is a gift not for Peter alone nor for the Twelve personally, nor even for their successors, but for the Church as a whole. The pope *participates* in that infallibility in a special way. The *Catechism of the Catholic Church* has a marvelous summary of infallibility in paragraph 891.

Long before infallibility was *formally* defined, the Fathers and Doctors of the Church understood that the pope had this gift. In A.D. 449, Saint Peter Chrysologus, a Doctor of the Church (c. 400–450), encouraged a fellow bishop to "heed obediently what has been written by the Most Blessed Pope of the City of Rome; for Blessed Peter who lives and presides in his own see provides the truth of faith to those who seek it. For we by reason of our pursuit of peace and faith, cannot try cases on the faith without the consent of the Bishop of the City of Rome."[2] In the thirteenth century, Saint Thomas Aquinas held that the pope "is empowered to decide matters of faith finally, so that they may be held by all with unshaken faith".[3]

From the very first century, popes themselves spoke with the assumption that their authority was final. Peter did so when he excused the Gentiles from the requirement of circumcision and proclaimed it to the whole Church (Acts 10—11:15). Saint Clement of Rome (88–96) did so when he authoritatively exhorted the Corinthians. Pope Saint Damasus I (c. 366–384) did so when he said, "The holy Roman Church has been placed at the forefront not by the conciliar decisions of other Churches, but has received the primacy by the evangelic voice of our Lord and Savior."[4] Pope Leo I regarded his Tome as the final word on the dual nature of Christ when he had it read at the Council of Chalcedon in 451 (see Peter Speaks on p. 60). Recognizing the singular authority of the popes *was not later invention*; it was acknowledged and exercised *from the very first century*.

The specific manner in which papal infallibility is exercised was defined at the First Vatican Council in 1870:

> we teach and define as a divinely revealed dogma that when the Roman Pontiff speaks EX CATHEDRA, that is, when, in the exercise of his office as shepherd and teacher of all Christians, in virtue of his supreme apostolic authority, he defines a doctrine concerning

---

[2] Peter Chrysologus, *Letter* 25.2, in *The Faith of the Early Fathers*, trans. W. A. Jurgens (Collegeville, Minn.: Liturgical Press, 1979), 3:268.

[3] Thomas Aquinas, *Summa Theologiae* II–II, q. 1, a. 10.

[4] Damasus I, *Decree of Damasus* 3, in William A. Jurgens, trans., *Faith of the Early Fathers*, vol. 1 (Collegeville, Minn.: Liturgical Press, 1978), pp. 406–7.

Peter Speaks Through Pope Leo the Great

"But [Jesus'] birth in time has taken nothing from, and added nothing to, that divine eternal nativity, but has bestowed itself wholly on the restoration of man, who had been deceived: that it might overcome death and by its own virtue overthrow the devil who had the power of death. For we could not overcome the author of sin and death, unless he had taken our nature and made it his own.... For just as the [deity] is not changed by his compassion, so the man[hood] is not swallowed up by the dignity [of the Godhead]. Each nature performs its proper functions in communion with the other." (Leo I, *Letter 28 to Flavian* [June 13, 449] in *Leo the Great, Gregory the Great*, ed. Philip Schaff and Henry Wace, trans. Charles Lett Feltoe, vol. 12 of *A Select Library of the Nicene and Post-Nicene Fathers of the Christian Church* [New York: Christian Literature, 1895], pp. 39–40)

faith or morals to be held by the whole Church, he possesses, by the divine assistance promised to him in blessed Peter, that infallibility which the divine Redeemer willed his Church to enjoy in defining doctrine concerning faith or morals. Therefore, such definitions of the Roman Pontiff are of themselves, and not by the consent of the Church, irreformable.[5]

---

[5] Vatican Council I, Dogmatic Constitution on the Church of Christ *Pastor Aeternus* (July 18, 1870), no. 4, https://www.ewtn.com/library/councils/vi .htm#6.

Based on the practice and teaching of the Church from time immemorial, the definition makes several important statements:

- Infallibility as applied to the pope is divinely revealed and is part of the deposit of faith.
- It consists of defining that a belief concerning faith or morals is held by the universal Church. The word *definition* here means a statement that authoritatively brings to an end any legitimate dispute about what the Church believes.
- It applies only when the pope speaks officially as "shepherd and teacher of all Christians". In other words, it is always an *explicit* exercise of his authority as successor of Peter, not simply as an individual theologian, bishop, or patriarch.
- It involves the assistance of the Holy Spirit.
- An infallible definition cannot be reversed and does not require the consent of the Church.

So, what can the pope define infallibly? Primarily, he can define what applies to our faith. For example, the pope can infallibly define that Jesus is physically present in the Eucharist, or that God is a Trinity.

Secondarily, he can define those facts needed to protect the deposit of faith or to explain it. For example, he can state that a particular book does in fact teach heresy. Or he can canonize a saint, which elaborates the communion of saints that is part of the deposit of the faith (Rev 19:6–9).

There are limitations to what the pope can infallibly pronounce. For example, he is not infallible when he speaks on facts of history or theories of science, unless these matters are connected to the deposit of faith. The pope couldn't define that a theory of physical evolution is true, because that has nothing to do with the deposit of faith. He could, however, state that God uniquely created the first human couple, because such a statement is connected with revelation.

It is clear what infallibility *is*. Unfortunately, people sometimes confuse it with a few things that it *isn't*.

First, infallibility is often confused with *inspiration*. Scripture is *inspired* because what the authors have written is "God-breathed"—God is the primary author (*CCC* 105–8). Inspiration is a *directive* action of the Holy Spirit. Infallibility, on the other hand, is a *protective* mechanism that guards against error—a very important distinction.

The Church makes no claim that God "breathes into" papal teaching. The Church doesn't even claim that the pope has a good sense of timing, that his definition says all that needs to be said, or that his meaning is clear, just that what he says isn't wrong. Infallibility only claims that the Holy Spirit protects the Church from being led into error in matters of faith or morals.

Second, infallibility doesn't mean that the pope is *impeccable* (unable to sin). Peter called himself a sinful man (Lk 5:8), and he did sin by denying Jesus. Yet Jesus gave Peter an infallible teaching office, indicating that the Spirit would lead him into all the truth. The pope is not sinless—he goes to confession regularly. The charism of infallibility does not protect the pope from sin, only from teaching error when he defines a matter.

Third, infallibility doesn't mean that *everything* the pope says or does is infallible. The definition of infallibility clearly lays out specific conditions: he must speak explicitly in the fullness of his papal office to define a matter of faith or morals. It's not enough for him to speak as a theologian, or as a local bishop, or even as patriarch of the

West. He must speak officially, without compulsion, as the head of the universal Church.

And this brings us to noninfallible teaching. Are Catholics free to dissent from them, or disregard them? In a word—no.

Vatican II is clear that "religious submission of mind and will must be shown in a special way to the authentic magisterium of the Roman Pontiff, even when he is not speaking ex cathedra".[6] At the very least, Catholics need to give the Magisterium the benefit of the doubt if they question a specific nondefined teaching. As Cardinal Newman pointed out, understanding of doctrines develops over time.[7] Even popes grow in understanding as they apply the gospel to new situations. But Catholics are not free to reject noninfallible teaching out of hand if they don't like it.

The pope is the head of the Church's Magisterium. The presumption among Catholics *must* be that the Magisterium understands the faith. As Vatican II puts it, the pope's "supreme magisterium [must be] acknowledged with reverence, the judgments made by him [be] sincerely adhered to, according to his manifest mind and will." And how do we recognize what the pope's mind and will are? They "may be known either from the character of the documents, from his frequent repetition of the same doctrine, or from his manner of speaking".[8]

---

[6] Vatican Council II, Dogmatic Constitution on the Church *Lumen Gentium* (November 21, 1964), no. 25, http://www.vatican.va/archive/hist_councils/ii_vatican_council/documents/vat-ii_const_19641121_lumen-gentium_en.html.

[7] See John Henry Newman, *An Essay on the Development of Christian Doctrine*, in *Conscience, Consensus, and the Development of Doctrine*, ed. James Gaffney (New York: Doubleday Image Books, 1992), pp. 86–101.

[8] Vatican II, *Lumen Gentium*, no. 25.

Why the Pope Teaches

Why all of this papal teaching? Paul, charging Timothy to keep "certain persons" from teaching error, myths, or their own speculations (1 Tim 1:3–4), tells us why: "The aim of our charge is love that issues from a pure heart and a good conscience and sincere faith" (1 Tim 1:5). In the same way, the pope wants to make sure that we are holy and in love with God.

Error, myth, and heresy have been concerns of popes from the beginning. In his second letter, Peter himself reminds Christians that he was not preaching myth when he presented the gospel. He wants them to remember the truth and learn to interpret scriptural texts accurately, especially the letters of Paul, so that the churches' faith might be stable (see Peter the Teacher on p. 65).

The pope regards protecting sound teaching as one of his primary mandates. In a 1993 General Audience, John Paul II remarked that the pope must "establish and authoritatively confirm what the Church has received and believed from the beginning, what the apostles taught, what Sacred Scripture and Christian Tradition have determined as the object of faith and the Christian norm of life."[9]

The pope teaches Catholics about their vocation to holiness of life. The Second Vatican Council made the connection between teaching and holiness:

> The Lord Jesus, the Divine Teacher and Model of all perfection, preached holiness of life to each and everyone of His disciples of every condition.... "Be you therefore

[9] John Paul II, General Audience (March 10, 1993), quoted in *The Roman Pontiff Is the Supreme Teacher: Catechesis by Pope John Paul II on the Church*, no. 4, Totus2us, 2017, http://www.totus2us.com/vocation/jpii-catechesis-on-the-church/the-roman-pontiff-is-the-supreme-teacher/.

Peter the Teacher Warns against False Teachers

"We did not follow cleverly devised myths when we made known to you the power and coming of our Lord Jesus Christ, but we were eyewitnesses.... And we have the prophetic word made more sure. You will do well to pay attention to this as to a lamp shining in a dark place, until the day dawns and the morning star rises in your hearts.... No prophecy of Scripture is a matter of one's own interpretation, because no prophecy ever came by the impulse of man, but men moved by the Holy Spirit spoke from God. But false prophets also arose among the people, just as there will be false teachers among you....

"So also our beloved brother Paul wrote to you according to the wisdom given him, speaking of this as he does in all his letters. There are some things in them hard to understand, which the ignorant and unstable twist to their own destruction, as they do the other Scriptures. You therefore, beloved, knowing this beforehand, beware lest you be carried away with the error of lawless men and lose your own stability." (2 Pet 1:16, 19–21; 2:1; 3:15–17)

perfect, even as your heavenly Father is perfect" (Mt. 5:48). Indeed He sent the Holy Spirit upon all men that He might move them inwardly to love God with their whole heart and their whole soul, with all their mind and all their strength (cf. Mk. 12:30).... Thus it is evident to everyone, that all the faithful of Christ of whatever rank or status, are called to the fullness of the Christian life and to the perfection of charity; by this holiness as such a more human manner of living is promoted in this earthly society.[10]

Reminding catechists that "the Church has always considered catechesis one of her primary tasks," John Paul II zeroed in on its main purpose: "to put people not only in touch but in communion, in intimacy, with Jesus Christ".[11] Nowhere is this point made clearer than in his challenges to the youth of the world. Speaking to a half million teenagers in Denver in 1993, John Paul II told them that listening to the pope means more than just being a "good person". He urged youth to get involved in "that never-ending battle being waged for our dignity and identity as free, spiritual beings."[12] He added: "Do not be afraid to go out on the streets and into public places like the first apostles who preached Christ.... This is no time to be ashamed of the Gospel.... It is the time to preach it from the housetops!"[13] To teenagers in Paris four years later, he made the connection between holiness and life: "Continue to contemplate God's glory and God's love, and you will receive the enlightenment needed to ... help our brothers and sisters to see the world transfigured by God's eternal wisdom and love."[14] At World Youth Days, held every two to three years,

---

[10] Vatican II, *Lumen Gentium*, no. 40.

[11] John Paul II, apostolic exhortation *Catechesi Tradendae* (October 16, 1979), nos. 1, 5, http://w2.vatican.va/content/john-paul-ii/en/apost_exhortations /documents/hf_jp-ii_exh_16101979_catechesi-tradendae.html.

[12] George Weigel, *Witness to Hope: The Biography of John Paul II* (New York: HarperCollins Cliff Street Books, 1999), p. 683.

[13] Ibid., p. 797.

[14] John Paul II, "Homily at the Mass for the 12th World Youth Day", Longchamp Racecourse, Paris, August 24, 1997, no. 6, http://w2.vatican.va/content /john-paul-ii/en/homilies/1997/documents/hf_jp-ii_hom_19970824_youth -paris.html.

the pope continues to encourage youth toward personal holiness and evangelization.

As Saint John Chrysostom said, Jesus "appointed Peter teacher of the world"![15] His successors have filled his office well, by the grace of God.

---

[15] John Chrysostom, *Homilies on the Gospel of St. John*, homily 88, in *A Library of Fathers of the Holy Catholic Church: Anterior to the Division of the East and the West* (Oxford: John Henry Parker; London: F. and J. Rivington, 1853), p. 793.

Chapter 4

The Pope as Gift to the Church and the World

"And I tell you, you are Peter, and on this rock I will build my Church, and the gates of Hades shall not prevail against it" (Mt 16:18). However much these words may have meant to Simon Bar-Jona, they go beyond him as an individual. To the Church, they are an ever-fresh promise—a prophecy. Peter lives in his successors, and Jesus is still building his Church upon him.

A buried acorn does not look like the mature oak tree sprung from it, but they are organically the same. Likewise, the Church hasn't always looked as it does now—neither has the papacy. Like the Lord who founded it, the Petrine office has grown "in wisdom and in stature, and in favor with God and man" (Lk 2:52). It also has suffered bouts of illness and come under attack from within the Church and without. But it always regained vigor, promoted holiness, and grew stronger with age. Peter *continues* to strengthen the brethren and feed Jesus' flock.

Here are the stories of several popes who have made great contributions to the Church and the world, both in range and in substance.

How Peter Set the Pattern

Imagine Jesus spending all night in prayer, and then announcing his vicar, the man who will carry the keys of his kingdom. Which would you choose if you were in his place?

Would you choose the brash and reckless bumbler who thinks too highly of himself? The one who speaks too soon, puts his foot in his mouth, and makes promises he can't keep? The disciple who asks you to explain the simplest parables, who tries to correct you in front of others, and lies to protect himself when he's in trouble?

Or would you choose the natural leader, the successful businessman? The one everybody mentions first? The one who speaks for the others—and, if he speaks wrongly, is willing to take the consequences? The one who risks what the others are afraid to? The one who, like many fishermen of Galilee, is devoutly religious and comes from a devout family? The one who can admit his own sinfulness (see Lk 5:8) and, when he falls, get up again? The one who's willing to ask you for help (Mt 14:30) and to exercise the authority you gave him to cast out demons and heal the sick (Mk 6:7, 13; Acts 3–4)? The one who, in the long run, is faithful and would leave his family, home, and business to follow you?

You may choose number two, but in reality the two alternatives are two sides of the same man, Simon Bar-Jona. He was the one Jesus picked and then nicknamed "Rock".

Simon was born in Bethsaida, on the east bank of the Jordan River as it feeds into the north end of the Sea of Galilee. The location is significant, because Greek and other Gentile cultures influenced Bethsaida and its neighboring towns.

Leaders of the Sanhedrin in Jerusalem regarded Simon Peter as uneducated and common. He was not trained as a doctor of the Law, but as a devout Jew, Simon may have attended religious school, learning enough Hebrew to read the Torah and the Prophets. It's clear that—especially after the Pentecost event—Simon understood the importance of the Law and the Prophets, for he often quoted Scripture when he spoke in public. But schooling must have ended for him in his teens, when he began to work full-time in the fishing trade.

The fishing business demanded patience, hard work, knowledge of fish and the sea, willingness to risk bad weather at night, and skill with boats and nets. It required teamwork, because the long dragnets had to be deployed and hauled in by at least two boats. Simon had to deal with markets and customers to negotiate a good selling price. He was a good businessman, made a good living, owned a home, and supported a family.

Luke hints that Simon met Jesus more than once before becoming a disciple (Lk 4:38–39). Healings and a miraculous catch of fish at Jesus' word may have finalized his commitment (Lk 5:1–11). Jesus knew he would change Simon's name the first time he met him (Jn 1:42). At the unique site of Caesarea Philippi, known for its huge rock wall, Jesus changed Simon's name to Kepha (Aramaic for *Rock*). This amazing site was the perfect backdrop for commissioning Simon as the rock upon which he would build his Church; and Jesus gave Peter the promise of the keys to govern it (Mt 16:18–19) (see Primacy of Peter on p. 72).

In Acts 1–15 we learn about Peter's leadership of the fledgling church in Jerusalem. But because of persecutions and the rapid expansion of the Church as a whole, Peter moved to Syrian Antioch, where the Gentiles rose to prominence in the Church. Later, as the gospel spread

How the Primacy of Peter Is Reflected in the New Testament

A snapshot can capture the image of a person. The New Testament captures the person and role of Peter.

In Luke 5, he's a fisher of men—a missionary. He's a boat captain, and his boat (or "bark") became a symbol of the Church that he pilots into deep water for a catch. He catches people from all lands and tongues, and in John 21 he hauls them ashore without the net tearing (schism).

In John 21, he's also the shepherd who feeds and tends (teaches and governs) Jesus' flock out of love. This image reflects a concern of the Church for papal leadership, pastoral care, and protection from heresy. Jesus prophesied Peter's crucifixion in John 21 and commanded him to "follow me" there.

To Matthew, Acts, and Paul, he is the Rock. On him, the Church is built. Peter is a "pillar" of the Church, part of the foundation of the New Jerusalem (Eph 2:19–20; Rev 21:14).

Finally, Peter is keeper of the keys of the kingdom of God. In Acts, he is the only one of the Twelve that speaks, and his name is used in the Gospels about four times more frequently than any other person except Jesus.

westward, he moved west, traveling and preaching in Asia Minor, through Corinth, and finally to Rome, where he led the universal Church until his death.

Though Peter was not called a *pope* during his lifetime— Leo I adopted that title in the fifth century, and Pope Saint

Gregory VII reserved it to the bishop of Rome in the eleventh (see Pope Saint Gregory VII below)—he *was* what the word means, a father to the Church. As the chief steward of the Israelite monarchy was referred to as a father

Pope Saint Gregory VII [Hildebrand] (1073–1085)

Hildebrand the monk lived in a time of decline for the Church. A string of weak popes allowed kings to appoint bishops for political reasons (a problem called "lay investiture"), and scoundrels with money to buy their way into bishoprics (the abuse called "simony").

Having served under five popes, he became pope in 1073 and took the name of his predecessor, Gregory the Great. Like his model, Gregory VII became a strenuous reformer, suppressing simony wherever he found it, promoting morality, and combating lay investiture.

Typical was Gregory's famous confrontation with the German king Henry IV. Henry wanted to keep bishops under his own control; Gregory reserved this right to the papacy. When the king threatened to resist by force, Gregory excommunicated him—a political as well as spiritual blow to Henry's prestige. Sincerely or not, Henry traveled as a barefoot penitent to Canossa in Northern Italy to meet Gregory. Suspecting a publicity stunt, the pope nonetheless restored him to communion.

Then the king did an about-face, appointed an antipope, and marched on Rome. Gregory's

(*continued*)

Pope Saint Gregory VII [Hildebrand] (1073–1085) (*continued*)

defense force was so undisciplined that the citizens of Rome drove the pope out of the city.

Though Gregory died in exile at Salerno, his efforts enabled the papacy of the Middle Ages to enjoy an independence from government interference. Henry's antipope, who called himself Clement III, hung on for sixteen years. Following Gregory's death, however, nearly a year passed before the cardinals elected a legitimate successor, Victor III.

Despite this, Gregory VII is one of the great reform popes. Reform popes are not usually popular, but the Church needs them. Gregory VII was one of the great reformers. He was canonized in 1606.

(Is 22:21), so the bishops of Rome became known as "pope" (Greek, *pappas*), or *father* of the faithful in God's kingdom. Paul notes that Peter's mission was primarily to the Jews, but the arrangement was fluid. It was important that Peter himself first open the door of faith to Jew and Gentile (Acts 10), oppose circumcision for Gentiles (Acts 15:7–11), and take responsibility for them at Antioch (Gal 2:11–21).

Peter set the pattern for his successors in three ways. First, the pope is to feed and tend the flock of Christ (Jn 21:15–17)—that is, to teach and govern the Church. Second, he is to strengthen his fellow apostles, the bishops (Lk 22:32). Third, he is to be a witness to the gospel even to the giving up of his life (Jn 21:18–19). Both Acts and Peter's letters show him discharging the first two of these commissions. He concludes his first letter: "I have written briefly to you, exhorting and declaring that this is the true grace of God; stand fast in it" (1 Pet 5:12). As for the last, history is clear that Peter was executed by crucifixion in Rome under Emperor Nero. All popes must stand ready for the same fate—the same witness.

Great Popes, and What Made Them Great

Only three popes have been given the title "The Great" (though many apply it to John Paul II as well). Two are ranked among the Latin Fathers of the Church—which means they were saintly, orthodox teachers whose doctrine had a shaping influence on the faith. But the Holy Spirit has raised up other great popes just when the Church needed them. Here are the stories of a few.

Saint Leo the Great (440–461)

Leo must have been furious when his two representatives returned from Ephesus in 449. He thought his letter to Flavian had settled the heresy that Jesus' humanity was swallowed up by his divinity. He also thought the council would clear things up, but events were manipulated so his letter was not even read during the proceedings.

The Second Council of Ephesus had been called by Emperor Theodosius in A.D. 449 to resolve new doubts about the faith that had surfaced since the first council there in A.D. 431. The doubts were spread by a monk named Eutyches, who claimed that Christ had two natures before the Incarnation but only one nature after the Incarnation, in a kind of fusion of his human and divine natures. Flavian, patriarch of Constantinople, denounced him as a heretic. Leo's dogmatic letter to Flavian (nicknamed the Tome)[1] was a long explanation of orthodox Church teaching, and he regarded it as final. Plus, it supported Flavian. But Eutyches had the emperor's ear, and the emperor made sure that "they" (the bishops who ran the council) would support the heretic Eutyches against Flavian—and Leo.

The pope responded by branding the council a "robber's council" and refused to recognize it. He called for a new council to be convoked in the West where he could oversee it. Instead, the emperor convened the new council at Chalcedon, near Constantinople. This time, Leo sent a stronger delegation and made sure that his letter was read at the second session. Seventeen times the bishops acclaimed it, most memorably in the outcry, "Peter has spoken through Leo!"

Still, some bishops resisted. To offset Leo's claim to speak for the whole Church, some Eastern bishops waited until the papal legates had left, then inserted a canon making Constantinople (the imperial capital) equal to Rome (an imperial has-been). Since Rome was not the most important capital city anymore, the bishop of Rome should not be the most important leader anymore. It was a weak argument, and Leo rejected it.

Leo had been thinking about why the bishop of Rome has the task of governing the universal Church even before these events in the East. He had served as a diplomat, lawyer, and deacon of Rome under three popes. This powerful position brought him face-to-face with two heresies from the West (Pelagianism and Manichaeism), and two from the East (Monophysitism and Nestorianism). He

[1] See John Jay Hughes, *Pontiffs: Popes Who Shaped History* (Huntington, Ind.: Our Sunday Visitor, 1994), p. 38.

was convinced that only papal authority could protect the faith everywhere from heresies like these—and he had the example of earlier popes to guide him. He needed to clarify the issue of papal authority. The question was, On what grounds?

Was the authority of the pope connected with Rome's status as the imperial city? Imperial cities come and go. Or was it tied to Peter's residence in Rome? Neither argument sufficed. As he pondered it, Leo hit on a simple analogy from Roman law that provided a much firmer explanation—inheritance.

What Jesus gave Peter was an office, as is made clear by Jewish precedent in the chief steward of the kingdom (Is 22). Peter's successor, in other words, inherits the office. This biblical understanding was also intelligible to those with a Roman background. According to author John Jay Hughes, "In Roman law the deceased lived on in the heir. The latter replaced the former and stepped into his shoes. At death the rights and duties of the deceased passed undiminished to his heir."[2]

The pope's authority doesn't rest on location but on an inherited office. Scripture pointed to the transition of authority, and Roman law illustrated how it worked. Leo knew he wasn't Peter. But as Peter's "unworthy heir" he had teaching and governing authority over the heirs of the other apostles. The unwavering defense of this view of papal primacy was mainly what made Leo a great pope. He helped to establish the biblical, theological, and legal grounds for the Church's understanding of the papal office.

Pope Leo had plenty of opportunity to exercise his authority. Many school children remember the story of him confronting Attila the Hun at Mantua in 452.

[2] Ibid., p. 30.

Diplomacy worked, and Attila withdrew. But three years later, the Vandal king Geiseric invaded Italy and was not inclined to be so gracious. Leo met him near Ostia, but the most Leo could do was persuade Geiseric not to burn Rome. Many popes since then have been forced to negotiate with rulers to protect the Church from military or political harm.

Leo I reigned as pope for twenty-one years. He is the first to call himself officially a *pope*, a father to the faithful. He died in November 461 and is buried in St. Peter's Basilica.

Saint Gregory the Great (590–604)

"In the salutation of your letter I find the selfsame pompous title, 'Universal Bishop,' that I forbade you to use." Gregory's pen scratched across the surface of the parchment. "I beseech your sweet Holiness not to repeat this."[3] Gregory paused in his letter to the patriarch of Alexandria. Universal bishop. Similarly, the patriarch of Constantinople wants to be called ecumenical patriarch, too, and pretend *he's* the universal bishop. A worthy man, but vain.

He resumed writing. "I want to be eminent not in words but in example. Nor can I consider something an honor which I know diminishes the honor of my brothers. My honor is the honor of the universal church."[4] He paused again. Not universal bishop, but servant. A servant of God's servants.

That's how Gregory I described his office, and how he lived it. He didn't deny his office or its authority. He maintained his unique authority as bishop of Rome, but

[3] Quoted in ibid., p. 47.
[4] Ibid.

carefully reminded other bishops that the main job of the bishop was service.

The Church has had its share of reluctant popes, but Gregory may have been among the most reluctant. Italy was sinking into civil chaos, with pagan Lombards raiding everywhere and the Eastern emperor too distracted with wars in the Balkans to help the West.

After serving ably as prefect of Rome, Gregory lived as a monk on one of his family's estates. But, with conditions as they were, Pope Pelagius II needed the young monk's experience. He ordained Gregory a deacon of Rome and then sent him as a papal delegate to the emperor in Constantinople to seek military aid. For seven years, he tried without success to obtain help. But he formed many friendships at court and came to know the Greek Church well.

Recalled to Italy, Gregory lived at his beloved monastery, but there was no seclusion there. Assigned by the pope to resolve a schism among northern bishops, he labored in vain to restore unity. Then disaster struck Rome. Floods destroyed much of the city's food supply and caused an outbreak of plague that took the life of the pope himself. In 590, Gregory was elected pope—over his own strenuous objections. He wrote a letter of protest to the emperor, but the emperor nevertheless confirmed the election.

So, the servant set about serving. Chronically ill—his own fasting had damaged his health—he set a pace of work that would exhaust an athlete.

In Gregory's day, the papacy owned a patchwork quilt of estates dotting the countryside from Gaul to North Africa, intended to generate money for the upkeep of the Church and to meet the needs of the poor. Gregory reorganized them and turned them into revenue producers. With that income, Gregory provided aid for plague victims and the starving of Rome and surrounding territories. The money also helped pay for a small military for the city's protection.

As civil government deteriorated, the bishops of Italy had to provide services that the government no longer could. Bishops fed the people, saw to government works such as building and road repair, provided for civil defense, and still ran the local church. Gregory was always on the lookout for men to ordain as bishops who were both good administrators and men of God. Though he didn't want to be a monarch, Gregory became, in effect, the ruler of most of Italy.

Gregory had an argument with the patriarch of Constantinople—the one calling himself "Universal Bishop". Gregory saw that title, as used by this patriarch, as a usurpation of papal authority and an act of pride. (To the patriarch it meant only that he had authority over the bishops in his jurisdiction.) By denouncing the term "Universal Bishop" and refusing such a title himself, Gregory did not deny the primacy of Peter's see—as his teachings and actions demonstrate. He was defending the real episcopal authority of all other bishops.

He wrote in his Epistle 68: "For if one, as he supposes, is *universal bishop*, it remains that you are not bishops."[5] Gregory tried in vain to get the patriarch to drop the title. Constantinople didn't budge, and the quarrel dragged on after Gregory's death. Despite this debate, Gregory believed devoutly in both papal primacy *and* the collegiality of all bishops.

[5] Gregory the Great, book IX, letter 68, in "Selected Epistles of Gregory the Great, Bishop of Rome (Books IX–XIV)", *Gregory the Great (Part II), Ephraim Syrus, Aphrahat*, ed. Philip Schaff and Henry Wace, trans. James Barmby, vol. 13 of *A Select Library of the Nicene and Post-Nicene Fathers of the Christian Church*, Second Series (New York: Christian Literature Company, 1898), p. 19.

When a door for the evangelization of the Anglo-Saxons opened in Britain, Gregory jumped at the opportunity. He sent Augustine and forty monks to England. He recommended ways to organize the Church there and made Augustine archbishop of Canterbury. Even though a pope, Gregory always wore his monk's habit and encouraged monasticism. Gregory was a tireless writer of letters (850 have survived), homilies (more than sixty still exist), Scripture commentaries, spiritual writings, and books—all of which made him one of the most widely read authors of the Middle Ages.

His spiritual teachings are very modern. Gregory challenged the notion that only certain religious souls could practice contemplative prayer. In a homily, he stated flatly that "anyone who keeps his heart in custody may also be illuminated by the light of contemplation."[6] It's the same call to holiness that Vatican II urges on the Church today.

Gregory I reigned for fourteen years. He is a great pope because his example set the standard of what the "complete pope" should be like. A newly elected pope who wanted to know how a pope should act had only to study Pope Gregory: his holiness, his communication skills, his government, his orthodoxy and readiness to expose heresy, and his evangelistic outlook. Strong medieval popes like Gregory VII (1073–1085) and Innocent III (1198–1216) (see Pope Innocent III on p. 82) were in the mold of Gregory I.

Pope Saint Pius V (1566–1572)

Europe—the heart of the Western world—was a mess. The Catholic world was disintegrating. Political alliances were collapsing, wars were erupting, and not even the pope was safe from attack. The Protestants had broken

---

[6] Jordan Aumann, *Christian Spirituality in the Catholic Tradition* (London: Sheed and Ward, 1985), p. 76.

Pope Innocent III (1198–1216)

The title "Vicar of Christ" had been used before, but not officially. Most of the time, the pope was called "Vicar of Peter". Innocent III disliked that title, since it implied the pope was Peter's, not Christ's, representative. "Vicar of Christ" also emphasized the pope's universal primacy. So he made the title official.

A century after Gregory VII, Innocent was still completing the reforms Gregory started. Elected in 1198, Innocent had other matters to deal with as well. He called two Crusades for the recapture of Jerusalem from its Muslim conquerors. Both failed, one incurring the enmity of the Orthodox with the sack of Constantinople in 1204. He also called for military action against the Albigensian heretics when they murdered his legate. That action, too, went awry as French barons used the occasion to grab power.

More successful was the Fourth Lateran Council, which Innocent called to restore unity with the Orthodox (the reunion was short-lived) and promote the Eucharist. Lateran IV defined the doctrine of transubstantiation. The council required Catholics to receive the Eucharist at least annually, hoping to encourage regular reception of Communion.

Innocent III died in 1216, after a reign of eighteen years.

with the Church and were themselves fragmenting, causing chaos in society. It appeared that truth, civil stability, and loyalty were shattering into a million fragments. Something had to be done.

Antonio Ghisleri entered the Dominican Order at age fourteen, the very year Luther published the *Ninety-Five Theses* (1517). He made his religious profession in 1521, the very year Luther's break with Rome became final. Ordained in 1528, Ghisleri was teaching philosophy and theology at Pavia when Henry VIII took over the English Church in 1534. Ghisleri was living in an age of tremendous religious conflict. Philosophy and theology were tools to sustain and explain the truth, and the Inquisition was a tool for exposing and preventing the spread of heresy. Ghisleri's zeal for the Church brought him into positions of leadership in exposing heresy.

His rise in Church affairs was rapid, though unwelcome to him. As a monk, he prized a simple life of poverty in the cloister. Pope Pius IV died in 1565; after a month-long conclave, the cardinals chose Ghisleri, who took the name Pius V. Unlike many of his recent predecessors, Pius wanted to live a holy life—and he wanted those around him to do so, as well. He continued the Dominican practice of poverty. He wore his white Dominican habit (thereby establishing the custom of popes wearing white cassocks). He walked barefoot and without a head covering in procession. He ate alone (the origin of another papal custom), woke early for prayer, and celebrated Mass daily. His holiness affected everyone who met him.

Most important, the pope's personal piety would have consequences for the entire Church. When Pius IV finally concluded the Council of Trent convoked eighteen years earlier by Paul III (see Pope Paul III on p. 84), the bishops breathed a sigh of relief. The council had accomplished much, but it had been an exhausting and even dangerous enterprise. Most of them were content to publish the acts of the council and return home. Only a few, like Charles Borromeo of Milan, actually began to implement council decisions. But the new pope

Pope Paul III (1534–1549)

As a young cleric, Alessandro Farnese lived a self-indulgent life. That began to change when he was ordained a bishop in 1509, and the shift gradually accelerated when he was elected pope in 1534. Calling himself Paul III, he realized the need to take the Protestant challenge seriously. He commissioned a study on the state of the Church that served as an action plan for the Council of Trent.

It was not easy to call such a council—the idea was not popular among bishops, and Italy was unstable. All the same, he gathered a small group of bishops at Trent. In seven sessions during his reign, they published documents on both dogma (Scripture and Tradition, justification, and the sacraments) and reform. The emperor Charles V interfered in the work of the council, prompting the pope to suspend the sessions until after the emperor's death.

Paul III was a strong reformer. The council he began strengthened Catholic doctrine and contributed to the Catholic Counter-Reformation. He approved new religious orders, most notably the Ursulines and the Jesuits. Paul died in 1549 after a reign of fifteen years.

knew that if the papacy didn't bring the council into the Church's life, its decisions would mean nothing.

With Borromeo's aid, Pius V spent the rest of his six-year reign implementing Trent from Rome to the Far East. He focused some of his attention on bishops. Unless no suitable candidate was available, Pius made sure that all bishops presided over only one diocese and actually lived there. He carefully appointed cardinals to help with Church administration. He helped establish and reform seminaries, as mandated by Trent in 1563. The pope also targeted catechesis. He published the *Roman Catechism*— the Church's only worldwide catechism until 1994— whose structure provided a model for the *Catechism of the Catholic Church*. The *Roman Catechism* is still in print. He oversaw the creation of the Roman Missal, which spelled out the rite of what is commonly called the "Tridentine Mass", used throughout the Latin Church for four hundred years. He made Thomas Aquinas a Doctor of the Church; thanks largely to Pius V, Aquinas enjoys a privileged position in Catholic theology.

It is often hard for a pope, as bishop of Rome, to take a direct concern for his own diocese. So many other global concerns press upon him. As part of his effort to implement the council, Pius V began a pattern of visitations to all the Roman basilica churches and arranged for other bishops to visit all the parishes in the diocese.

Pius V was a great pope because of his zeal for the integrity of the faith. He is the first pope to devote himself wholeheartedly into the implementation of such a wideranging reform as the Council of Trent. Pius V died in May 1572 and was canonized in 1712.

Pope Saint Pius X (1903–1914)

The cardinals wanted a pastor as pope. For centuries, popes had been either seminary professors or diplomats or both. Giuseppe Sarto had spent his priestly career in one pastoral position after another. He was an assistant pastor for nine years, a parish pastor for eight, a diocesan bishop for another nine, and cardinal patriarch of Venice for ten. Not only was he an effective shepherd of souls; he was reputed to work miracles—literally. The Church needed such a man.

Cardinal Sarto was elected pope in August 1903. Taking the name Pius, he used a passage from Ephesians as his motto: "To restore all things in Christ" (1:10). Pius wasn't thinking of restoration after a period of decline, for the papacy was gaining strength and the Church was rapidly expanding everywhere. The kind of restoration he had in mind was both pastoral and theological—he hoped to restore a living faith among the laity, and the integrity of doctrine among those responsible for teaching it.

Pius' greatness as a pope can be illustrated with two initiatives he took, one pastoral and one theological.

On the pastoral front, he attacked a problem that had plagued the Church for nearly thirteen hundred years. Since roughly the sixth century, inappropriately expressed respect for the holiness of the Eucharist or a sense of personal unworthiness had kept people away from Holy Communion. Repeatedly, popes and councils enacted and reinforced laws obliging the faithful to receive Communion at least once a year. Pius sought to broaden reception of Communion and encouraged all Catholics, even children as young as seven years old, to receive the Eucharist often, daily if they could.

In other progressive moves, Pius updated both the Roman Missal and the Breviary from which the Divine Office (now called Liturgy of the Hours) is said. He started the codification of canon law (though the first Code of Canon Law was not published until 1917, three years after his death). He also began the move to enlist more laity to help in the apostolic work of the Church. Pius was even in the vanguard of liturgical reform. In 1907, he published a document reforming Church music, establishing

Gregorian chant as the model for melodies and Scripture as the basis of musical texts.

On the theological front, Pius saw the need to shore up the deposit of faith for future generations. Once "queen of the sciences", theology had taken a back seat to modern—that is to say, nineteenth century—science, social engineering experiments, and atheistic philosophies. Theologians felt constrained to ground theology on the same sorts of methods and standards as the secular sciences. Since those viewed reality in terms of what could be observed, probed, and weighed apart from considerations of faith, theologians felt that they should attempt to do likewise. The result was what Pius X saw as a "synthesis of all heresies"—Modernism.[7]

Turn-of-the-century Modernism is a Catholic version of nineteenth-century liberal Protestantism. It was a complex phenomenon. Essentially, it took a "less is more" approach to faith. Though it came in many forms and did not have a unified set of teachings, in a general manner it taught that believers should rely on the following:

- Scientific assumptions, not revelation. Miracles aren't possible, because they violate the laws of nature. Thus, Jesus' Resurrection must be a "spiritual" reality, not a physical one.
- Experience, not authority. Modernism denied the divinity of Christ because the modern mind allegedly could not accept the idea of God becoming man. What people believe about God is based on their experience of the sacred.

---

[7] Pius X, *Pascendi Dominici Gregis* (September 8, 1907), no. 39, http://w2
.vatican.va/content/pius-x/en/encyclicals/documents/hf_p-x_enc_19070908
_pascendi-dominici-gregis.html.

- Values, not truth. Since no authority (Bible, Church, whatever) can tell people what to believe, it's up to each person to decide for himself. Truth is relative to the believer.

The pope identified sixty-five specific Modernist positions that Catholics could not accept. He excommunicated those who taught them and required that all priests, seminary professors, and religious superiors take an oath of fidelity. Unfortunately, Modernism reemerged tentatively in the middle of the twentieth century (when it was put down again by Pius XII), but reappeared in full strength after Vatican II. More than fifty years after the council, the Church is still dealing with various aspects of it.

Certainly, Pius X refused to compromise on essentials. A pastor at heart, he was holy in his own life and desired to make conditions right for everyone else to become holy. He was a fierce opponent of anything that threatened the integrity of the faith. He was even willing to sacrifice Church property in order to leave the Church free to preach the gospel. That happened in 1904 when the French government confiscated Church property because the pope wouldn't capitulate to its wishes. But that sacrifice secured the Church's independence from government control.

Pius X died at the outset of World War I, after a reign of eleven years. Pius XII beatified him in 1951 and canonized him three years later.

Pope Saint John Paul II (1978–2005)

It's as if he were invisible. Nobody seemed to see him. Not the Gestapo, who searched his apartment and missed him praying behind a closed door. Not the Russian army, which was executing anyone active in the Polish resistance. Not even the Polish Communist government,

Pope Saint John XXIII (1958–1963)

Most of the world thought that electing a seventy-seven-year-old cardinal to the papacy meant that John XXIII would simply be a caretaker pope. But John XXIII had other ideas. He knew that the Holy Spirit had work for him to do.

In 1958, Angelo Giuseppe Roncalli was elected pope—and soon announced that he would convoke the Second Vatican Council to deal with the Church's proclamation of the gospel to the modern world. His idea was to have all of the Church's twenty-eight hundred bishops discuss ways to update how the Church could proclaim its age-old message. He also changed the tone of the council to allow the bishops full freedom to discuss issues among themselves, and to deal with problems positively rather than through anathemas. The council also welcomed non-Catholic observers for the first time.

Beloved for his holiness and sense of humor, Pope John died in June 1963, after a reign of only five years. Pope John Paul II beatified him in 2000, and Pope Francis canonized him in 2014.

which thought he was harmless and let him be ordained bishop of Kraków. It's as if the Holy Spirit were protecting the man he would place in the Chair of Peter, where everyone could see him.

The Holy Spirit protected Karol Wojtyla's education as well as his safety. After high school, he and his father moved to Kraków, where Karol started classes at the Jagiellonian University. That didn't last long. The German military occupied Kraków, arrested professors, and shut the university down. Karol continued his education in secret, studying philosophy, theology, and languages. He also became active in underground theater—an activity that could get him shot.

In 1940, around the time of his father's death, Karol met Jan Tyranowski, a mystic from whom he learned the practice of interior prayer. He also became a seminarian under the cardinal archbishop of Kraków, Adam Sapieha. Following the war, when the Russian army was rounding up young men, Karol "disappeared" into the cardinal's residence, where he completed his seminary training and was ordained to the priesthood. The cardinal sent him to Rome, where he earned the first of two doctorates.

Back in Poland, Father Wojtyla disguised much of his pastoral work from the Communists as ethics lectures and camping trips (both for catechizing young people). He did pastoral work in two parishes and lectured at the Jagiellonian. In 1958, he became auxiliary bishop of Kraków and promptly made himself a thorn in the side of the government. When the Vatican Council opened in 1962 under John XXIII, Bishop Wojtyla attended, joining one of the planning commissions. Pope Paul VI appointed Wojtyla archbishop of Kraków in 1963, and four years later he made him the cardinal archbishop of that city. All the while, the new prelate was publishing his teaching on love, sexuality, and marriage—elements of what would later be called his "theology of the body".

There were two conclaves in 1978. Pope Paul VI died in August, and Pope John Paul I died a month after his election. Cardinal Wojtyla was elected in October—the first non-Italian pope in more than four hundred years and the first Polish pope ever.

He immediately broke protocol, receiving his brother bishops standing (instead of sitting), addressing the people in St. Peter's Square (instead of merely blessing them), and using the first person singular ("I" instead of the customary "we"). Like John Paul I, he was installed (instead of crowned) a week later and revealed a theme of his pontificate: "Be not afraid!"

John Paul II dedicated himself to an authentic implementation of Vatican II. To critics who complained that his orthodoxy was "opposed to the spirit of Vatican II", he distinguished *Tradition*—the handing on of the faith—from *traditionalism*, what one theologian called "the dead faith of the living".[8] An energetic pope, he commissioned the publication of the first universal catechism in four hundred years; affirmed the Church's moral teaching; developed catechesis on marriage and family life; confirmed the Church's stand on the male priesthood and her celibacy; defended the dignity of the human person from conception to natural death; defended human dignity from both Communist and capitalist oppression; reached out to Orthodox, Protestants, non-Christians, and even atheists; brought the gospel to the world's youth; launched the New Evangelization; and prepared for the Third Millennium and the Great Jubilee. Those, for starters.

John Paul II began to travel to every continent and most countries, drawing crowds numbering in the millions. Though he was an old man, youth flocked to him and his teaching. He went where he was sometimes not welcome and disarmed criticism by unaffected humility. He pushed open further the door of communication with the Orthodox. He met with religious leaders from most major non-Christian religions and prayed with them.

---

[8] Jaroslav Pelikan, *The Vindication of Tradition: The 1983 Jefferson Lecture in the Humanities* (New Haven, Conn.: Yale University Press, 1984), p. 65.

Pope John Paul II died shortly after Easter in 2005, was beatified by Pope Benedict XVI in 2011, and was canonized by Pope Francis in 2014. He has been hailed by popular acclamation as Pope Saint John Paul the Great. According to biographer George Weigel, "no human being in the history of the world has spoken to so many people, in so many different cultural contexts"[9]—or in so many different languages. John Paul II became the first pope with a *personal* global outreach.

From Saint Peter through the current pontiff, all popes have been united by the awareness that the papacy is a witness to Christ's presence in the world. In *Crossing the Threshold of Hope*, John Paul II wrote: "One duty of the pope is to profess this truth and to render it present to the Church in Rome as well as to the entire Church, to all humanity, and to the entire world."[10] (See Core Teaching on pp. 92–93.)

Core Teaching on Popes in the *Catechism of the Catholic Church*

"When Christ instituted the Twelve, 'he constituted [them] in the form of a college or permanent assembly, at the head of which he placed Peter, chosen from among them' (*LG* 19). Just

(continued)

---

[9] George Weigel, *Witness to Hope: The Biography of Pope John Paul II* (New York: HarperCollins Cliff Street Books, 1999), p. 844.

[10] John Paul II, *Crossing the Threshold of Hope* (New York: Alfred A. Knopf, 1994), p. 14.

Core Teaching on Popes in the *Catechism of the Catholic Church* (*continued*)

as 'by the Lord's institution, St. Peter and the rest of the apostles constitute a single apostolic college, so in like fashion the Roman Pontiff, Peter's successor, and the bishops, the successors of the apostles, are related with and united to one another' (*LG* 22).

"The Lord made Simon alone, whom he named Peter, the 'rock' of his Church. He gave him the keys of his Church and instituted him shepherd of the whole flock. 'The office of binding and loosing which was given to Peter was also assigned to the college of apostles united to its head' (*LG* 22 § 2). This pastoral office of Peter and the other apostles belongs to the Church's very foundation and is continued by the bishops under the primacy of the Pope.

"The Pope, Bishop of Rome and Peter's successor, 'is the perpetual and visible source and foundation of the unity both of the bishops and of the whole company of the faithful' (*LG* 23). 'For the Roman Pontiff, by reason of his office as Vicar of Christ, and as pastor of the entire Church has full, supreme, and universal power over the whole Church, a power which he can always exercise unhindered' (*LG* 22)." (*CCC* 880–82)

Chapter 5

The Selection of the Pope

Most people think a new pope is the successor of the pope he *replaces*. Therefore, Francis is the successor of Benedict XVI, who was the successor of John Paul II.

But that is not all there is to it. The pope is *not* just the successor of the previous pope. He is the successor of *Peter*—Peter the Apostle.

How did the selection of popes in the early Church take place, how did the selection process evolve, and how does it work today? And what is the significance of the black and the white smoke?

Peter and His Early Successors

In chapter 4, we learned some of the reasons *why* Jesus chose Peter to lead the Church. Jesus apparently had several reasons. Peter was a natural leader. He was outspoken (a trait the Holy Spirit could refine), flexible, and humble enough to accept Jesus' corrections. He had hope, a hope that carried him through the guilt of his betrayal— a hope Judas lacked. He had faith, enough to walk on the water. He had love, enough to lay down his life for Jesus. But Jesus also chose Peter because Peter had received the revelation from God identifying who Jesus really was (Mt 16:15–18).

We also know *how* Jesus chose Peter. He appointed him, as any king would appoint his chief steward.

Peter's appointment may have been the model for appointing Peter's first successors. The New Testament refers several times to apostles appointing elders of churches, through the laying on of hands. Possibly, the first four popes were appointed by their predecessors. We know very little of the selection process in the first century, but if the early popes were appointed by their predecessors, it appears that in the early second century the appointment of the bishop of Rome ended following the pontificate of Alexander I.

Evolution of the Conclave

After A.D. 105, popes appear to have been elected. Selection of the pope meant selecting the bishop of Rome, so the election was restricted to Rome and its immediate vicinity. Everybody in that Christian community was involved, including neighboring bishops, Roman clergy, and even laity. The clergy would choose a candidate, and then the laity would affirm the choice by acclamation.

In the fifth century, Pope Leo I modified this method somewhat (creating the custom of having the current pope make rules for the selection of the next pope). Under Leo's plan, the community would provide a list of nominees. The laity and clergy together would shorten the list, and then the clergy and local bishops would make the final selection.

From the sixth to the tenth centuries, secular rulers, political dignitaries, military officials, and prominent families began interfering in papal elections to get their own favorites elected. Attempts to appease or to get around the interference would cause long delays between elections, and when an election finally took place, the process could last months. Also, the city of Rome often erupted in riots following an unpopular decision.

Pope Nicholas II (1059–1061) made cardinals responsible for the papal election. Under this plan, neighboring dioceses submitted the names of candidates and then cardinal priests narrowed down the list of choices. Cardinal bishops made the final choice. The Roman clergy and laity could approve, but their role was passive.

The Third Lateran Council (1179) ruled that a two-thirds majority of cardinals was needed to elect the pope. But since the council didn't say how quickly the election had to occur after the papacy became vacant, a long time might pass between the death of a pope and the next election. Getting the necessary majority could take a while, too. The longest papal election ever took nearly three years (1268–1271). Eventually, the frustrated citizens tore off the roof of the papal palace where the cardinals were meeting, locked them inside, and restricted them to a diet of bread and water. The election of Gregory X followed quickly.

That solution created the conclave—a meeting of the College of Cardinals for the purpose of electing a pope. Gregory liked it so much that he enshrined it in Church law (see Longest and Shortest Conclaves on p. 98).

At that time, cardinals could elect a pope by acclamation. But that method fell into disuse; the last pope to be elected by acclamation was Gregory XV (1621–1623). If no one garnered a two-thirds majority vote, the cardinals could "compromise" by selecting a small, odd-numbered group of cardinals to do the voting for everyone else. But that method removed responsibility from the whole College of Cardinals, and recently has been forbidden.

Longest and Shortest Conclaves

The election of Gregory X lasted more than two years and nine months. In 1274, Pope Gregory mandated in the bull *Ubi Periculum* that elections start within ten days of a pope's death. Plus, the cardinal electors were to be locked in with a key (*cum clave*, thus *conclave*); and the longer it took to elect a candidate, the more their food, outside contacts, and income would be restricted. A couple of subsequent popes abandoned the idea, but it was soon restored with minor changes.

The shortest conclave seems to have been the first one after Gregory's death (1276). It lasted only a day and resulted in the election of Innocent V.

With the emergence of absolute monarchies in the sixteenth century, various governments tried to steer the outcome of papal elections in their favor. They claimed the right to tell their cardinals whom to vote for from a list of likely candidates, or to promise to abide by government vetoes. The problem came to a head at the conclave of 1903, when the Austro-Hungarian emperor vetoed the results of a ballot. But by then, the cardinals had had enough. Upon his election, Pius X outlawed the veto, placing papal elections entirely in the hands of the cardinals (see Veto on p. 99).

Traditionally, a conclave takes place when a pope dies. But a papal resignation would also prompt a conclave. Celestine V (1294), Gregory XII (1406–1415), and Benedict XVI (2005–2013) all resigned for various reasons, and Francis has hinted that resignation is a possibility for him.

Veto at the Conclave of 1903

Leo XIII died on July 20, 1903. One cardinal likely to be elected at the conclave was Cardinal Rampolla, Leo's secretary of state. When the vote on August 2 favored the cardinal, the cardinal archbishop of Kraków announced Emperor Franz Josef's veto. The cardinals, including Rampolla, protested the veto, and went on with the voting. On the seventh vote, the two-thirds majority favored Giuseppe Sarto of Venice. He took the name Pius X and the motto "To renew all things in Christ". That renewal included doing away (in January 1904) with a supposed right of a secular government to intervene in papal elections. The pope also mandated automatic excommunication for any cardinal that would try to exercise or even threaten the veto.

During WWII, Pius XII made provisions that if he were taken prisoner by the Nazis, he would resign so that a new pope could be elected rather than let the Nazis use him as a hostage. While papal resignations have been rare in Church history, Benedict XVI's resignation suggests that they could become more common.

The Selection Process Today

The cardinal who summons the conclave is the chamberlain of the papal household (*camerlengo* in Italian). When a papal vacancy occurs, he manages the process of electing the new pope. If the pope has died, he must confirm that death has truly taken place, destroy the pope's ring and seals (lest they be misused), and close the papal apartments. (The same procedure is followed if the pope resigns.) The chamberlain also announces the pope's death publicly and arranges the funeral.

When a conclave becomes necessary, the papal chamberlain summons the cardinals to Rome from all over the world. The conclave begins between fifteen and twenty days later. His job is so crucial that one of the new pope's first actions is to appoint a papal chamberlain.

The conclave always takes place in the Sistine Chapel, starting with the hymn *Veni Creator Spiritus* ("Come, Creator Spirit"). At each vote, the cardinals write the name of a candidate on a paper ballot, fold it, and walk up to a special chalice to deposit it. As they drop the ballot into the chalice, they swear an oath that the man they are voting for is the person they believe the Holy Spirit wants elected. If no candidate receives a two-thirds majority, the ballots are burned in a special stove with wet straw, producing black smoke coming out of the chimney. The cardinals then proceed to another vote. Once a candidate receives a two-thirds majority, the ballots are mixed with dry straw, producing white smoke. The world then knows that we have a new pope!

Thereupon, the chamberlain asks the elected cardinal if he accepts the election and, if so, what name he wishes to take (see Popes on p. 101). If he is a bishop, the new pope assumes office the moment he accepts his election. If he is not yet a bishop, he must be consecrated a bishop first; then he becomes pope upon ordination. (This provision is largely hypothetical; no nonbishop has been elected pope in a very long time.)

Popes tend to take a close interest in the procedures for the election of the next pope. Seven popes in the

Popes Who Changed Their Names

The first pope to change his name was John II (533–535). His given name was Mercury, the name of a pagan god. He changed it to John in honor of Pope John I (523–526), who had been imprisoned by Theodoric, king of Italy.

Another noteworthy name change was that of Sergius IV (1009–1012). His given name was Peter di Porca. He disliked being called Peter II, however (Peter I being the apostle), so he took another name.

Usually, a pope takes the name of a predecessor he admires, or whose policies or pastoral vision he wishes to continue (though he may select another name, as Jorge Bergoglio did by choosing the name Francis after Saint Francis of Assisi; there was no previous pope of that name). The change of name also reflects a total commitment to the office.

The use of double names began with Albino Luciani, who took the name John Paul I (1978) to honor Pope John XXIII (1958–1963) and Pope Paul VI (1963–1978). John Paul I lived only a month after his election, however. When Karol Wojtyla was elected, he took the same double name for similar reasons, becoming John Paul II.

twentieth century have written guidelines for the selection of a successor. Under John Paul II, for example, the rules include the following.

First, the methods of acclamation and compromise, described earlier, are out. Both were too subjective or unwieldy. The election must be made by secret ballot.

The two-thirds rule still applies unless a protracted dead-lock emerges, in which case a simple majority may be used. (In 2007, Pope Benedict XVI rescinded the simple majority rule.)

Second, the election must take place in the Sistine Chapel, the traditional location for the last four hundred years.

Third, as in the past, the electors are secluded and the proceedings are kept secret. The new rules, though, add some modern touches: no letters, phone calls, e-mails, faxes, newspapers, or televisions are allowed within the area set aside for the election. And the Sistine Chapel is to be inspected for bugging devices.

Fourth, before voting, the cardinals must listen to two talks on the current problems facing the Church and the need for careful discernment in the selection of the new pope. Like the popes before him, John Paul II urged electors to make their choice freely before God and apart from personal friendships and political concerns.

Finally, cardinal electors no longer have to sleep in temporary cells. They will be housed—under strict surveillance—in St. Martha's Residence, a lodging for visiting clergy that can accommodate 130 guests. (Paul VI decreed in 1975 that cardinals who reached the age of eighty were ineligible to vote in the conclave, and that the number of cardinal electors would be limited to 120.)

Above and beyond the human efforts, the Holy Spirit is at work in these conclaves. It is the promise of Jesus to be with his Church until the end of time, and his inti-mate involvement with the Church is very much realized in the election and oversight of the pope.

Chapter 6

The Pope as Brother to Others

Pope John XXIII once greeted a group of Jewish visitors saying, "I am Joseph, your brother."[1] Typical of him, the greeting was a joke, a play on his own name (Giuseppe, or Joseph). It also alluded to the Genesis story when the patriarch Joseph revealed his identity to his brothers, the sons of Jacob or Israel (Gen 45:4).

Pope John's greeting was no nicety of protocol. It signaled his intentions as pope to be a brother in deed as well as word both with Jews and non-Catholic Christians. Two years before the opening of the Second Vatican Council, Pope John established the Secretariat for Christian Unity. As preparations for the council advanced, he had a document prepared on relations between Christians and Jews, hoping to eradicate any vestige of anti-Semitism in the Church. That was the origin of the 1965 Vatican II document *Nostra Aetate* (Declaration on the Relation of the Church to Non-Christian Religions).

---

[1] *L'Osservatore Romano* (October 19, 1960); translation of the article by *L'Osservatore Romano* that reports on the meeting can be found on the website of the Council of Centers on Jewish-Christian Relations at http://www.ccjr .us/dialogika-resources/documents-and-statements/roman-catholic/second -vatican-council/naprecursors/1259-j2319600ct19. Pope John XXIII also included this remark in his encyclical *Ad Petri Cathedram* (June 29, 1959), no. 90, http://w2.vatican.va/content/john-xxiii/en/encyclicals/documents/hf _j-xxiii_enc_29061959_ad-petri.html.

Since the council, popes have continued to promote better relations with other Christians and with non-Christians. Since John XXIII, popes have been clearing the way for dialogue with Eastern churches (Orthodox), separated brethren (Protestant communions), non-Christian religions (Jews, Muslims, Buddhists, and others), even the world at large (see Pope as World Leader below).

The Pope as World Leader

The pope not only leads the Church as her pastor and chief teacher; he is also the head of a small but influential state. In such a dual and significant role, he has important relationships with the world's religious and political leaders.

The pope has been a political leader for most of Christian history, beginning with the collapse of the Western Roman Empire when the pope had to step in and fill the void. This step did not result from a desire of popes to assume power as political leaders. Rather, it became necessary to restore order and leadership as secular governments abandoned their role. Papal intervention helped preserve order, religion, culture, and civilization. During the Middle Ages, the papal government owned and managed lands in Italy and elsewhere, originally given to the Church as land grants when the Roman Empire declined. Governing these territories made the pope a monarch, who used revenues to help the poor of Rome and worked with leaders of neighboring countries as peers, in peace and in war.

(continued)

The Pope as World Leader (*continued*)

As late as the nineteenth century, the Papal States (as they were called) included sixteen thousand square miles of land and more than three million people. These states dwindled until only the city of Rome remained as the pope's territory—and even that was lost to the Italian government in 1870. The Lateran Treaty of 1929, negotiated by Pope Pius XI, resulted in some financial compensation for the loss of territory. More important, it established Vatican City as a sovereign state with the pope as its sovereign, a move designed to protect the Church from antagonistic forces within the Italian state. In 1948, the treaty was reconfirmed and incorporated into the Italian constitution. And in 1985, it was modified to separate the Church from the Italian state more completely than before.

As head of this small state, the pope has continued to play a significant role on the world's political stage. In 1964, the Vatican under Paul VI joined the United Nations as an observer nation. Though it has no voting rights, the Holy See has exerted its influence to resist the efforts of more developed countries to force aggressive population control programs, including sterilization and abortion, on developing nations. At times, the Holy See has been called upon to help settle armed conflicts. John Paul II had a major role in the collapse of the Soviet Union and European Communism. The Holy See maintains full diplomatic relations with many countries, including the United States and Israel.

The Eastern Churches

Most Catholics from Europe, Africa, and the Americas belong to the "Western Church"—the Latin Rite. They may not realize that the Catholic Church includes twenty-three different ritual churches, collectively called "Oriental" or "Eastern" Catholic churches. These include the Byzantine (Greek), Chaldean (Iraqi), Maronite (Lebanese), Coptic (Egyptian), Malabar (Indian), and several other particular churches. All are Catholic, and all are in union with the bishop of Rome. Their members are Catholic but not *Roman* Catholic. Only members of the Roman Rite are Roman Catholics. Members of other ritual churches would be Byzantine Catholics, Chaldean Catholics, Maronite Catholics, and so forth.

These Eastern Catholic churches are not the same as the Eastern Orthodox churches, which lack union with the pope. Nevertheless, "the Eastern Churches in communion with the Apostolic See of Rome have a special duty of promoting the unity of all Christians, especially Eastern Christians" not in communion with Rome.[2] Because they retain hierarchical structures, liturgies, and theological traditions almost identical to those of Eastern Orthodox Christians, the Eastern Catholic churches are in the best position to help forge the path to reunion with the See of Rome.

But that's easier said than done—the divisions run long and deep.

What caused the divisions? Several factors. One significant factor was *culture*. Despite their union in the Christian

[2] Vatican Council II, Decree on the Catholic Churches of the Eastern Rite *Orientalium Ecclesiarum* (November 21, 1964), no. 24, http://www.vatican.va/archive/hist_councils/ii_vatican_council/documents/vat-ii_decree_19641121_orientalium-ecclesiarum_en.html.

faith, the Greek-speaking East and the Latin-speaking West had different ways of thinking about law, custom, ecclesial relationships, and even theology. Language barriers only made matters more difficult.

Politics was another factor. As the center of imperial government shifted eastward, the Church at Constantinople (where the emperor was) saw its importance in terms of the center of government. But as imperial power vacated the West, the bishops of Rome recognized that the authority of their office did not come from Rome as a capital city, but from the fact that Rome was the place where Peter established his successors.

Still another factor was the slowness of *travel* and *communication*. A lot could—and did—happen between the time a sailing ship left one port with a message and when it put into port in another land.

The two *theological* issues usually credited for the split were the jurisdictional primacy of the papacy and the *filioque*. The Latin word *filioque* means "and the Son". It was added to the Nicene Creed, which originally read, "We believe in the Holy Spirit who proceeds from the Father". The West added "and the Son" to the end of this article, and the East accused the West of not involving them in such an important inclusion in the Creed.

Taken separately, none of these factors *caused* the Orthodox schism. The Church stayed unified for a thousand years in spite of the problems. But matters came to a head in 1054 when a Latin papal delegate and a Greek patriarch excommunicated each other. Leaders on both sides tried to repair the damage, but the wounds went deep. Both sides gradually sank into de facto separation. (One often hears that the Eastern churches split with the West in 1054, which is the date of the final excommunication declared by both sides. The final break of that year was the result of a series of developments that generated a long, slow separation over two hundred years in the making.)

Since then, the Orthodox East has developed into a set of loosely connected churches divided along national lines, many of them subject to the ruler or ideology that governs the territory.

Two Church councils (both held in the West) tried to restore union—and briefly achieved it. The Second Council of Lyons (1274) secured the allegiance of the ruler of Constantinople, but his clergy and laity of the East didn't want reunion. The Council of Florence (1431–1435) ended in agreement among theologians on both sides, especially about papal primacy. But the old hostilities—and pressure from Islam, which feared that the West would come to the military aid of the East—drew most of those communions away from Rome again.

Papal outreach to the Orthodox revived in earnest under Pope John XXIII. Both he and Paul VI made several overtures to Athenagoras I of Constantinople. Pope Paul especially tried to get ecumenical dialogue moving with the Orthodox after Vatican II ended. Subsequent popes have accelerated contacts between themselves and Eastern patriarchs, and have not balked at resistance or criticism from either side. Comparing the Eastern churches to Christianity's "other lung", John Paul II hoped "the Church [would] breathe with her two lungs" in the new millennium.[3]

The Protestant Communions

"Bible-believing" Protestants and other non-Catholic Christians readily admit that in Jesus there is "one body ... one Lord, one faith, one baptism" (Eph 4:4–5). But not all

[3] John Paul II, *Ut Unum Sint* (May 25, 1995), no. 54.

of them are willing to follow that logic further—that there is one Church. "Christ bestowed [unity] on His Church from the beginning. We believe that this unity subsists in the Catholic Church as something she can never lose, and we hope that it will continue to increase until the end of time."[4]

When Protestants do refer to the "unity of the Church", it often means an "invisible unity", a vague kind of brotherhood of those who have accepted Christ as their Savior. Since the unhappy time that Martin Luther broke with the Church and sparked the tragic fragmentation of much of Christendom, Protestants have devised a new tradition, abandoning much that was passed on by the apostles and the Fathers of the Church.

In two documents, the Second Vatican Council teaches that baptism brings all Christians into a form of union, even if an imperfect union, with the Catholic Church. *Lumen Gentium* admits that "the Church recognizes that in many ways she is linked with those, who being baptized, are honored with the name of Christian".[5] The document cites more than a dozen ways this joining appears in daily life. Since Jesus founded only one Church, *Unitatis Redintegratio* continues, "It remains true that all who have been justified by faith in Baptism are members of Christ's body, and have a right to be called Christian, and so are correctly accepted as brothers by the children of the Catholic Church."[6] As Christ's appointed head of all Christians,

[4] Vatican Council II, Decree on Ecumenism *Unitatis Redintegratio* (November 21, 1964), no. 4, http://www.vatican.va/archive/hist_councils/ii_vatican_council/documents/vat-ii_decree_19641121_unitatis-redintegratio_en.html.

[5] Vatican Council II, Dogmatic Constitution on the Church *Lumen Gentium* (November 21, 1964), no. 15.

[6] Vatican Council II, Decree on Ecumenism *Unitatis Redintegratio* (November 21, 1964), no. 3.

then, the pope has a responsibility even for those Christians not in full communion with the Church.

The "ecumenical movement" began among Protestants to promote Christian unity. But Protestants tend to have a different definition of ecumenism from that of the Church. Thus, ecumenism is the "working together" of various denominations and sects, but it rejects a visible, hierarchical Church as an option. Catholics, on the other hand, see true ecumenism as all Christians gathering together again in one visible Church, sharing one Eucharistic meal in one "house". Since the Second Vatican Council, the Catholic Church has been fully engaged in such efforts. And here again, the pope is taking the lead.

Pius XII opened the door to Catholic participation in ecumenical discussions and meetings in 1949. John XXIII invited representatives of Protestant communions to participate in the Second Vatican Council—and nearly one hundred did. John XXIII also established the Secretariat for Christian Unity, and he was the first pope to engage an Anglican archbishop in ecumenical dialogue. Christian unity was close to Paul VI's heart as well, and it was under him that *Unitatis Redintegratio* was promulgated. Pope Paul continued dialogues with the Anglicans and attended the World Council of Churches meeting in Geneva.

For many years, the Catholic Church has received Anglican and certain Protestant clergy into the Church, dispensing individuals from the norm of clerical celibacy for ordination to the priesthood on a case by case basis. Early in the current century, several bishops of the Church of England, unhappy with liturgical and moral changes in that communion, sought some kind of group-level incorporation into the Catholic Church, in such a manner that would preserve many elements of their Anglican spirituality and worship. In 2009 Pope Benedict XVI responded in the apostolic constitution *Anglicanorum Coetibus* by erecting personal ordinariates (similar to dioceses). Three of these ordinariates had been officially created by January 2012.

John Paul II invested heavily in ecumenical efforts, mainly through patient conversation and dialogue rather than by pushing for dramatic breakthroughs. Unity, he emphasized, must be based on the "adherence of all to the content of revealed faith in its entirety". After all, who would "consider legitimate a reconciliation brought about at the expense of the truth?"[7]

It is the calling of every Catholic to pray and work to heal the divisions and help our separated brethren to rediscover the fullness of the faith in the Catholic Church.

Judaism

Christianity emerged from Judaism as its Messianic fulfillment. Jesus' thinking was infused with the Hebrew Scriptures—he quoted them constantly. Mary, Joseph, and the Twelve were devout Jews. For almost the first decade, nearly all Christians were Jews.

Catholic liturgy represents a Christianized fulfillment of Jewish worship. In the Mass, the Liturgy of the Word has similarities to a synagogue service, and the Liturgy of the Eucharist is the fulfillment of a Passover meal. Sacraments such as matrimony and holy orders also have deep Jewish roots. And the Liturgy of the Hours is similar to the Jewish practice of setting aside certain hours of the day for prayer.

Despite the birth of Christianity in a Jewish context, the two faiths parted ways before the end of the first century. For nineteen hundred years, little was done to bridge

[7]John Paul II, *Ut Unum Sint*, no. 18.

the gap. In fact, up to the eve of World War II, many Christians persecuted Jews and were openly anti-Semitic. It took the horror of the World War II *Shoah* (Holocaust) to shock Catholics into looking again at their origins: "I am Joseph, your brother," said Pope John XXIII to Jewish visitors. But even earlier, on September 6, 1938, Pius XI had asserted, "Anti-Semitism is unacceptable. Spiritually, we are all Semites."[8]

Responding to Pope John XXIII's desire for a document on Catholic relations with the Jews, the Vatican Council produced *Nostra Aetate*. It reminded Catholics of their spiritual bond with Judaism and stated: "The Church, mindful of the patrimony she shares with the Jews and moved not by political reasons but by the Gospel's spiritual love, decries hatred, persecutions, displays of anti-Semitism, directed against Jews *at any time and by anyone*."[9] The document rejected anti-Semitism outright as "foreign to the mind of Christ".[10]

Follow-up documents discussed approaches to establishing dialogue with Jewish leaders, especially in general teaching and education. The International Catholic-Jewish Liaison Committee was established in 1971, discussing virtually every aspect of relations between the two religions. In 1985, the Vatican released guidelines on how to preach and teach about Jews and Judaism in a manner consistent with Catholic doctrine.

Since then, popes have done even more to raise the consciousness of both religions. In dozens of statements and talks; in meetings with Jewish leaders; in visits and pilgrimages to Jewish synagogues, holy sites, and monuments;

---

[8] Pius XI, *La Documentation Catholique* 29 (1938), col. 1460.

[9] Vatican Council II, Declaration on the Relation of the Church to Non-Christian Religions *Nostra Aetate* (October 28, 1965), no. 4; emphasis added.

[10] Ibid., no. 5.

and in public rebukes of Catholic complicity in anti-Jewish persecution, the popes are fostering fraternal relationships with Judaism and the Jewish people through words and deeds. Pope Benedict XVI was the first pope to invite Jews to his installation. Pope Francis communicates with the chief rabbis of Rome and Israel and enjoys lifelong relationships with the Jewish community.

Pope Pius XII, the pope during Nazi occupation of Italy, has been the victim of a smear campaign in recent years, but historians have exposed the smear campaign for what it is. To settle the debate over the role of Pius XII concerning Jews in World War II, John Paul II opened Vatican archives for research.

(The *Catechism of the Catholic Church* addresses the Catholic teaching on relations with the Jewish people in paragraph 839.)

Islam and Other Religions

From Islam's beginnings in the seventh century, most Christians regarded it as a threat. In the first century of its existence, Muslim warriors conquered half of Christendom. Islam virtually wiped out Christianity in Northern Africa, took over the entire Middle East, and for centuries threatened to overrun Europe. War between Muslims and Christians was nearly continual until the Christian victory at Lepanto in Greece in 1571.

Despite hostilities and religious differences with the Christian West, Islamic culture affected the development of European culture, as Islamic culture had been influenced by ancient Greek and Eastern Christian civilizations into which it came into contact as a result of conquest. Medieval Muslim scholars preserved texts of ancient Greek philosophers and developed a philosophical system of their own, which Christian philosophers engaged and debated, initially using Latin translations of Arabic translations of ancient philosophical works. At its zenith, medieval Islamic culture developed ideas in mathematics, astronomy, and science that influenced the advancement of these fields in the Christian West. Our numbering system, for example, is based on the Arabic system. Since the fifteenth century, developments in the West, such as the emergence of modern science and greater political and religious freedom, have added to the divergence between European civilization and Islam. The global spread of European-originated culture, including its technological advances, has affected Islam.

The Qur'an has been interpreted by some Muslims as teaching a limited respect for Christianity as a religion "of the book", and for Jesus and Mary—although the Qur'an's view of Jesus differs radically from that of Christianity. Although Islamic nations have severely punished conversions to Christianity (for example, conversion is still a capital offense in most Islamic countries), there are a few "secular" Islamic nations that allow Christians to practice their faith openly, but this is becoming less the case. The Open Doors USA World Watch List 2018, which tracks worldwide Christian persecutions, reports that eight out of the top ten countries and the large majority of the top fifty countries on the list are the result of Islamic oppression, and this oppression is continuing to spread.[11]

Nostra Aetate pleaded "with all to forget the past and to work sincerely for mutual understanding and to preserve as well as to promote together for the benefit of all

[11] Open Doors USA, World Watch List 2018, p. 4, https://www.open doorsusa.org/wp-content/uploads/2018/01/WWL2018-BookletNew.pdf.

mankind social justice and moral welfare, as well as peace and freedom."[12] Accordingly, recent popes have set up structures of dialogue and have teamed up with Islamic leaders to achieve mutual aims—for example, to resist enforced population control measures by antifamily constituencies in the United Nations. Popes since John Paul II have made it clear that improved relations with Islam are a priority. Since Vatican II, the popes have generally emphasized what they regard as the positive aspects of Islam and minimized its negative aspects. The resurgence of militant Islam has posed challenges to such an approach. While some Islamic leaders participate in interreligious dialogue, other elements in Islam aggressively oppose it. As is often the case in interreligious relations, those who could contribute the most to eliminating violence are the least inclined to talk.

Vatican II also acknowledged that other religions, particularly Hinduism and Buddhism, contain elements of truth (despite the many elements of error they also contain) (see *Catechism* on Church Relations on pp. 116–17). "The Catholic Church rejects nothing of what is true and holy in these religions," says *Nostra Aetate*. In fact, it urges Christians to enter with "prudence and love" into dialogue and cooperation with them, and to "recognize, preserve and promote the good things, spiritual and moral", they live out.[13]

The Church doesn't forget the need for zealous missionary work. Some Catholics have neglected to preach the gospel to believers of non-Christian religions. Paul VI reminds the Church that the call to preach Jesus as the world's only Savior is *not* optional. "This message is indeed

[12] Vatican II, *Nostra Aetate*, no. 3.
[13] Ibid., no. 2.

The *Catechism* on the Church's Relations with Other Religions

Non-Catholic Christians

" 'The Church knows that she is joined in many ways to the baptized who are honored by the name of Christian, but do not profess the Catholic faith in its entirety or have not preserved unity or communion under the successor of Peter' (*LG* 15). Those 'who believe in Christ and have been properly baptized are put in a certain, although imperfect, communion with the Catholic Church' (*UR* 3). *With the Orthodox Churches*, this communion is so profound 'that it lacks little to attain the fullness that would permit a common celebration of the Lord's Eucharist' (Paul VI, Discourse, December 14, 1975)." (*CCC* 838; emphasis in original)

Jews

"*The relationship of the Church with the Jewish People*. When she delves into her own mystery, the Church, the People of God in the New Covenant, discovers her link with the Jewish People, 'the first to hear the Word of God' (*Roman Missal*, Good Friday 13: General Intercessions, VI). The Jewish faith, unlike other non-Christian religions, is already a response to God's revelation in the Old Covenant. To the Jews 'belong the sonship, the glory, the covenants, the giving of the law, the worship, and the promises; to them belong the patriarchs, and of their race, according to the flesh, is the Christ' (Rom 9:4-5); 'for the gifts and the call of God are irrevocable' (Rom 11:29)." (*CCC* 839)

(*continued*)

The *Catechism* on the Church's Relations with Other Religions (*continued*)

Muslims

"*The Church's relationship with the Muslims.* 'The plan of salvation also includes those who acknowledge the Creator, in the first place amongst whom are the Muslims; these profess to hold the faith of Abraham, and together with us they adore the one, merciful God, mankind's judge on the last day' (*LG* 16)." (*CCC* 841)

Other Religions

"The Catholic Church recognizes in other religions that search, among shadows and images, for the God who is unknown yet near since he gives life and breath and all things and wants all men to be saved. Thus, the Church considers all goodness and truth found in these religions as 'a preparation for the Gospel and given by him who enlightens all men that they may at length have life' (*LG* 16)." (*CCC* 843)

"In their religious behavior, however, men also display the limits and errors that disfigure the image of God in them: 'Very often, deceived by the Evil One, men have become vain in their reasonings, and have exchanged the truth of God for a lie, and served the creature rather than the Creator. Or else, living and dying in this world without God, they are exposed to ultimate despair' (*LG* 16)." (*CCC* 844)

"To reunite all his children, scattered and led astray by sin, the Father willed to call the whole of humanity together into his Son's Church. The Church is the place where humanity must rediscover its unity and salvation." (*CCC* 845) necessary. It is unique. It cannot be replaced. It does not permit either indifference, syncretism or accommodation. It is a question of people's salvation."[14] He goes on:

> Even in the face of natural religious expressions most worthy of esteem, the Church finds support in the fact that the religion of Jesus ... objectively places man in relation with the plan of God, with His living presence and with His action.... In other words, our religion effectively establishes with God an authentic and living relationship which the other religions do not succeed in doing, even though they have, as it were, their arms stretched out towards heaven.[15]

The pope concludes that "the whole Church is missionary, and the work of evangelization is a basic duty of the People of God."[16]

[14] Paul VI, *Evangelii Nuntiandi* (December 8, 1975), no. 5, http://w2.vatican.va/content/paul-vi/en/apost_exhortations/documents/hf_p-vi_exh_19751208_evangelii-nuntiandi.html.

[15] Ibid., no. 53.

[16] Ibid., no. 59, quoting Decree on the Church's Missionary Activity *Ad Gentes* (December 7, 1965), no. 35: AAS 58 (1966), p. 983.

Chapter 7

Ten Common Attacks on the Papacy

Anti-Catholic attacks on the papacy run the gamut from challenging the underlying theology to attacking what the pope says and does. Here are ten of the most common accusations and the facts that answer them.

On the Role of the Papacy in Doctrine

Accusation: *The Pope can change doctrine.*

The Facts: No one, not even the pope, can change the content of divine revelation. That includes both written Tradition (Scripture) and oral Tradition (the teaching of the apostles).

As head of the Church's teaching office (Magisterium), the pope is responsible for safeguarding the full deposit of faith, which includes judging what is in fact divinely revealed. But the pope can neither add to that deposit nor take away from it—nor can he change it. His job is to protect it, to explain it, and to promote it. What the pope may change is the way a doctrine is formulated, or expressed. For example, the term *transubstantiation* tries to capture in one word what happens during the transformation of elements in the Eucharist. The content of the doctrine is that the elements really change at the Consecration—that fact can't change. The formulation is the word used to describe it—and that can develop over time to help clarify how we understand the fact.

In his ordinary teaching, the pope may apply scriptural or natural law principles to questions that the writers of Scripture had not envisioned (for example, genetic engineering and cloning). Neither Scripture nor the Fathers addressed these issues, but the Church applies established principles to new situations. The pope often uses teaching documents such as encyclicals to address such matters.

A clear distinction exists between dogma and discipline. Dogma can never change; Church discipline can and does change—as granted by the authority given to the Magisterium to bind and loose (Mt 16:19; 18:18).

Accusation: *The fact that popes have said things that are incorrect shows that they are not infallible.*

The Facts: Infallibility does not apply to everything the pope says. It only applies when the pope is explicitly engaging his infallibility by issuing an *ex cathedra* statement.

The truth of a papal definition does not depend on the pope's mere assertion of it, nor does something untrue suddenly become true after he speaks. The pope defines a doctrine because it is true and because for some reason a definition has become necessary. Infallibility is a gift of the Holy Spirit given to the Church, the "pillar and bulwark of the truth" (1 Tim 3:15). Primarily, infallibility is a negative protection; in other words, it prevents the Church from ever binding the consciences of the faithful to believe error.

Most papal teaching (in audiences, homilies, and most written documents) does not claim to be infallible. That's not to say that the teaching may be disregarded. Even when the pope is teaching noninfallibly on a matter of faith and morals, the presumption is that his teaching is correct and reliable (cf. *CCC* 892).

Accusation: *The sinfulness of some popes shows that they are not infallible.*

The Facts: If that were true, no one could be pope, because all eligible candidates are sinful. Jesus didn't use sinlessness as a criterion when appointing Peter to tend his flock. Though Peter denied him three times, Jesus restored and reinstated him by asking three times if Peter loved him. Peter's replies were followed with the commands: "Feed my lambs.... Tend my sheep.... Feed my sheep" (Jn 21:15, 16, 17).

There is a vast difference between infallibility and impeccability (inability to sin). The pope is not impeccable. Infallibility protects the pope from erring when, speaking as shepherd and teacher of all the faithful with the full weight of his apostolic authority, he intentionally and formally defines a matter. In Scripture Jesus promised to lead the Church "into all the truth" (Jn 16:13) and that "the gates of Hades shall not prevail against it" (Mt 16:18). That includes protecting the Church from error in teaching. It says nothing about preventing leaders of the Church from sinning.

On the Pope as a Person

Accusation: *The Church cannot be founded on Peter, because other passages say that someone else is the foundation.*

The Facts: This accusation assumes that a figure of speech ("foundation") can have only one application. But in

Scripture, the same figure can have several meanings depending on context. For example, in Matthew 16:18, Peter is the foundation rock and Jesus is the builder; but in 1 Corinthians 3:11, Christ is the foundation and Paul is the builder. Paul refers to Jesus as the foundation of the Church; but in Ephesians 2:20 and Revelation 21:14, all the apostles are the foundation. In its various images and examples, the New Testament refers to both Jesus and the apostles variously as the builders and the foundations.

It's not "either this meaning or that, but not both." Rather, both meanings are true. The image of a foundation applies in different senses to Jesus, to Peter, to the apostles together, or even to the content of the faith. In 1 Corinthians, Paul speaks about one apostle building on the foundation that another laid. In Peter's first letter, the context is moral behavior, the Person of Jesus being the foundation of all holiness. In Matthew, the context is Peter's office and his role of binding and loosing. The image of the Church's foundation captures all these meanings without contradiction. Scripture uses various figures of speech, and one should not confuse and mix them up.

Accusation: *Paul's rebuke of Peter (Gal 2:11–21) shows that Peter lacked authority in the early Church and was not infallible.*

The Facts: Paul rebuked Peter for a bad example, not a false teaching. He was challenging Peter for not living up to his authoritative teaching at the Jerusalem council (Acts 15:6–11). If Peter were not an authority, it would have been pointless for Paul to mention the correction to the Galatians. But in fact, Paul corrected Peter precisely because Peter's authority set him before everyone as a model of behavior. Paul also referred to Peter in this passage as *Cephas*, respectfully recognizing Peter as the "Rock" (*kepha* in Aramaic).

Paul isn't the only one to have corrected a pope. When Saint Catherine of Siena reproved Pope Gregory XI (1370–1378) for living in Avignon instead of Rome (his diocese), he returned to Rome. Catherine was later made a Doctor (teacher) of the Church.

In Galatians, Paul raised the issue for a reason. The Council of Jerusalem had settled the circumcision debate by removing some obligations of the Mosaic Law. But some Jewish converts in the Galatian church wanted to obligate Gentiles to circumcision, rather than to faith in Christ. Paul acknowledges that Peter himself knew this (Gal 2:16). In fact, Acts shows Peter defending this truth (Acts 10–11, 15).

In the second century, Tertullian wrote about this passage in Galatians saying, "The fault [of Peter] certainly was one of procedure and not of doctrine."[1]

Accusation: *Paul wrote far more books of Scripture than Peter, which shows that Peter was not the chief apostle.*

The Facts: The first half of the statement is correct. Paul was a highly educated Pharisee, trained by one of the best rabbis in Judaism at the time. It would be surprising if he had not written eloquently. Peter was a hands-on leader, a doer rather than a literary man. Most people of his day didn't read or write, so it isn't surprising that the fisherman Peter preached and engaged in pastoral work more than he wrote.

---

[1] Tertullian, *The Prescriptions against the Heretics* 23.10, in William A. Jurgens, trans., *The Faith of the Early Fathers*, vol. 1 (Collegeville, Minn.: Liturgical Press, 1978), p. 121.

The second half of the statement doesn't follow from the first. Importance isn't measured by literary output. The Apostle James was the third most important of the Twelve after Peter and John (Mt 17:1; Mk 5:37; 9:2; 14:33; Lk 8:51; 9:28). But he wrote nothing we know of and died early in Church history (Acts 12:2). We're blessed to have what Paul wrote. But in fact, he deferred to Peter and sought his approval to ensure that he was not working in vain (Gal 2:2).

On the Pope and His Power

Accusation: *James, not Peter, was head of the Jerusalem church.*

The Facts: Some have suggested that James the Just (author of the Letter of James) was head of the Jerusalem church because of his role in Acts 15. But Scripture nowhere states that James was its head, and it is clear from the early chapters of Acts that Peter was the leader of the Christian community there. By chapter 12, Peter had moved on "to another place" (12:17) to escape Herod, who knew of Peter's importance, but more importantly, to spread the good news of Jesus Christ by establishing the Church in new areas of the Roman Empire. According to Clement of Alexandria (d. 215), Peter, John, and John's brother James appointed James the Just to head the Jerusalem church so they could minister elsewhere. Peter was the teacher of the world, not just of Jerusalem. Further, during the Council of Jerusalem in Acts 15, James merely suggested pastoral provisions to help implement the basic theological determination that Peter had already announced under his authority as keeper of the keys.

Accusation: *The existence of antipopes shows a break in the line of popes. Therefore, today's pope cannot be a legitimate successor of Peter.*

The Facts: Jefferson Davis was president of the Confederate States of America during the Civil War. Had he claimed to be president of the *United* States of America, his claim would not have *made* him president. That office belonged to Abraham Lincoln. Nor would such a claim have broken the line of elected American presidents. When Secretary of State Alexander Haig claimed to be "in charge" after President Reagan was shot in 1981, his claim was well-intentioned, but false. The Constitution puts the vice president in charge if the president is incapacitated.

A false claim doesn't make one a true pope. Even though false claims may cause confusion for a time (as they did in the fifteenth century, when three men claimed to be the pope), they are still false claims and do not interrupt the line of genuine successors any more than false claims made regarding other offices. Ultimately, Jesus promised that his Church would endure (Mt 16:18; 28:20) regardless of disputes about who rightfully sits in the Chair of Peter.

Accusation: *The popes are sinning by not selling off all the Vatican's riches to feed the poor.*

The Facts: Judas used that argument when he accused Lazarus' sister Mary of extravagance in "wasting" precious perfume on Jesus (Jn 12:3–5). Jesus answered by saying that the poor would always be around, but the "waste" was well spent upon him.

The argument suggests that it is sinful to "waste" resources on God. If so, it was sinful of God to command the building of the Ark of the Covenant and the Tent of Meeting in such lavish fashion (Ex 25–28), or to sanction the building of a gorgeous Temple in Jerusalem (1 Chron 22, 28–29). The building of ornate temples and cathedrals can express a good and holy love of God, who is first and always deserves the best of what we have (Mal 1:6–9; Ex 23:10; Deut 18:4). Jesus welcomed Mary's "waste", for he predicted that the story would be told everywhere the gospel was preached.

The "riches of the Vatican" are mythological. The physical assets of the Church are in the form of buildings, libraries, hospitals, and other goods that can't readily be converted to cash. As to treasures like precious art and rare manuscripts, these items were donated in trust by Catholics around the world for their preservation and to share the history and glory of our faith with future generations. When it comes to liquid assets—cash—the Church relies on donations from Catholics everywhere and operates on a very tight budget. According to the CIA World Factbook, total expenditures for the Holy See in 2013 amounted to $348 million[2]—that's less than the budget of some *towns* in America. Even if the Church were to liquidate all assets and spend her entire operating budget on the poor of the world, it would make less than a ripple and would leave the Church nothing to work with in her *primary* endeavors, such as the worship of God and evangelization.

Accusation: *The popes have sinned by assuming temporal power (for example, over the Papal States) rather than keeping to purely spiritual affairs.*

The Facts: Scripture doesn't support that accusation. In ancient Israel, spiritual and temporal power were united,

---

[2] "The World Factbook: Europe; Holy See (Vatican City)", Central Intelligence Agency, accessed December 8, 2017, https://www.cia.gov/library /publications/resources/the-world-factbook/geos/print_vt.html.

as they were under Moses, Joshua, and the Judges, who apportioned land and waged war. After the Maccabean revolt against the Greeks, the High Priest took over temporal governing authority, which continued to some degree even under the Roman occupation (Acts 9:1–2; 23:5).

When Jesus told the Pharisees to "render therefore to Caesar the things that are Caesar's, and to God the things that are God's" (Mt 22:21), he was not implying that what belonged to Caesar didn't also belong to God. Scripture draws no clear line between temporal rule and "purely spiritual affairs" because each impinges on the other. The notion that the two can be separated, as some think the American Constitution tries to do, is a modern idea, based on political theories of the sixteenth and seventeenth centuries. It did not exist in the seventh century when Pope Gregory I was virtually forced by civil collapse to take over civil governing authority. Nor did it exist in the eighth, when King Pepin handed over to the pope lands confiscated by Lombard invaders. Since the Church is a visible society that operates in space and time, and since the Bible doesn't forbid religious leaders to exercise temporal power, it is lawful for popes to exercise a measure of temporal power, such as the government of Vatican City.

Chapter 8

The Pope and Your Catholic Life

At recent World Youth Days, popes have encouraged the young generation to listen to them as they prepare to take up their roles in the world. In Compostela, Spain, in 1989 John Paul II told his young audience, "Do not be afraid to be saints! This is the liberty for which Christ has set us free."[1] Building on this message, Pope Francis at Kraków in 2016 encouraged youth, "Dear young friends, don't be ashamed to bring everything to the Lord in confession, especially your weaknesses, your struggles, and your sins. He will surprise you with this forgiveness and his peace. Don't be afraid to say 'yes' to him with all your heart, to respond generously and to follow him!"[2]

World Youth Days have been among the largest gatherings of human beings in human history, and young people *are* listening to the pope. Wherever World Youth Days have taken place, bishops and pastors notice a remarkable increase in church attendance, in vocations, and in spiritual health. For example, researchers following up on the

[1] John Paul II, "Homily at the 4th World Youth Day", Monte del Gozo, Compostela, Spain, August 20, 1989, w2.vatican.va/content/john-paul-ii/en/homilies/1989/documents/hf_jp-ii_hom_19890820_gmg.html

[2] Francis, "Homily at World Youth Day", Campus Misericordiae, Kraków, Poland, July 31, 2016, https://w2.vatican.va/content/francesco/en/homilies/2016/documents/papa-francesco_20160731_omelia-polonia-gmg.html.

effect of the Sydney, Australia, World Youth Day in 2008 reported large increases in religious understanding, commitment, and practice among attendees.[3] The same phenomenon seems to have taken place wherever the World Youth Days have been held.

Listening to the Pope

Cynics allege that the pope doesn't know what is going on in the world, that he is behind the times, or that he is out of touch with political or theological reality. One sometimes hears that a pontiff so different in origin and cultural outlook and so insulated within Vatican walls can't understand the local cultures.

Obviously, the pope is a human being and therefore limited. His position may be part of that limitation. This coin has two sides, however—the pope's position can also serve as one of his greatest assets. The fact is, he is one of the best-informed leaders in the world with one of the most efficient communication networks on the planet. That was true even when the pope spent almost all his time at the Vatican and rarely traveled. It is even truer now that the pope travels frequently and comes into direct contact with local peoples everywhere.

One also must remember that in the first century Christianity was already a multiethnic communion. That didn't stop Saint Peter—a Jew from Galilee—from serving as the spiritual leader of Christians from diverse lands and cultures.

Not everyone likes what the pope says. His teachings often make people uncomfortable since the truth is often

[3] Andrew Singleton, "The Impact of World Youth Day on Religious Practice", *Journal of Beliefs and Values* 32, no. 1 (April 2011): 57–68.

painful. His teachings apply the gospel to current situations. Since the gospel itself always runs counter to the spirit of the age, the pope's words may be "hard sayings"—and they tend to be resisted even before they're fully heard. This is nothing new. Not only their enemies but also many who claimed to be brothers viciously opposed Peter and the other apostles.

When *Humanae Vitae* was published in July 1968, dissent began even before its official release. Reaction to the encyclical caused Pope Paul VI great personal anguish, yet he never backed down. Refusal to abide by this papal teaching is having disastrous consequences for society.

Papal documents are not always easy reading. Yet Catholics everywhere are hungry for authentic doctrine. John Paul II wrote *Veritatis Splendor* in 1993 to help Catholics understand and accept the moral teachings of the Church. That encyclical explains reasons for our moral choices and has generated intense interest among Catholics everywhere. The basic message is simple: morality is not a matter of one's personal opinion, much less merely a personal decision. It is a matter of *objective truth*, truth that can be discerned by the conscience through the natural law and revelation. Human beings have the responsibility to form their consciences according to the truth.

"Listening to the pope" means paying attention to what he is teaching. He speaks on issues of greatest importance to the whole Church. A given pontiff may not speak to each issue as many might think he should, or people may not agree with his position on debatable issues. Even so, Catholics should hear him with an attitude of deference and docility. The pope demonstrates daily a great concern about family, marriage, human dignity, respect for life, morality, authority—all issues that we Catholics face every day.

Is the pope concerned only with doctrinal matters? No, he is also deeply concerned about holiness and the love of God. The Church and the world need virtuous heroes in a culture spiraling into darkness and immorality. These heroes—saints—cut across lines of age, gender, culture, race, politics, and marital status. In an age when many people think there is "nothing worth dying for", the pope is especially interested in martyrs, men and women who witnessed to Christ with their blood.

"We have the mind of Christ," says Saint Paul (1 Cor 2:16). By reading documents from the Vicar of Christ, we learn not only what the Church teaches, but why— we learn how the Church *thinks*. So it becomes easier to think with and like Christ.

Following the Pope

A Roman centurion—a pagan—asked Jesus to cure his servant from afar, without having to enter his house. The centurion reasoned that Jesus could cure the servant from any location because he had authority from God to do it. The centurion knew about authority; he wielded it but was also under it. Jesus expressed delight: "Not even in Israel have I found such faith" (Mt 8:10; Lk 7:9).

Like the centurion, the pope also wields authority and is under it. He's subject to the authority of Christ, both personally and as a servant of the truth. He wields authority as the Vicar of Christ by teaching, governing, and sanctifying; and the Church—including each of us individually—responds by hearing, obeying, and growing in holiness. When a Catholic resists or rejects the pope's authority, he faces disastrous consequences. Jesus told the apostles, "He who hears you hears me, and he who rejects you rejects me, and he who rejects me rejects him who sent me" (Lk 10:16; cf. Mt 10:40; Jn 13:20).

Does that mean that Catholics can never criticize the pope? Not at all. Saint Paul criticized Saint Peter for acting according to a double standard (Gal 2:14). Saint Catherine of Siena criticized Pope Gregory XI (1370–1378) for living at Avignon instead of in his diocese at Rome. Saint Thomas Aquinas would go a little further.

> If the faith were endangered, a subject ought to rebuke his prelate even publicly. Hence Paul, who was Peter's subject, rebuked him in public, on account of the imminent danger of scandal concerning faith, and, as the gloss of Augustine says on Galatians 2:11, "Peter gave an example to superiors, that if at any time they should happen to stray from the straight path, they should not disdain to be reproved by their subjects."[4]

When Pope Benedict XVI published his three-volume *Jesus of Nazareth* in 2007, he said that people were free to criticize his work, since it was "in no way an exercise of the Magisterium".[5] Criticism of the pope should never arise out of a mere reaction to something he says or does. If possible, criticism should be informed by knowledge of the facts and from a position of respect—communicated through proper ecclesiastical channels.

Following the pope gives assurance that you are on solid moral and spiritual ground. It's not a question of being "conservative" or "liberal" or something else; it's a matter of truth. In his exercise of the Magisterium, the pope

[4] Thomas Aquinas, *Summa Theologica* II-II, q. 33, a. 4, New Advent, http://www.newadvent.org/summa/3033.htm.

[5] Benedict XVI, *Jesus of Nazareth*, vol. 1, *From the Baptism in the Jordan to the Transfiguration* (New York: Doubleday, 2007), xxiii–xxiv.

speaks as head of the Church, with a teaching authority from Christ himself (and the responsibility that goes along with it). You can't go wrong by following him.

When Paul VI upheld Church teaching on contraception, he warned that abandoning Church teaching would result in sexual promiscuity, the treatment of women as sex objects, divorce, and the failure of governments to protect marriage and family. His warning has come true. Catholic couples that ignore Church teaching on contraception have marriages that fail at similar rates to those in the rest of the population. By contrast, the pope promised that those who follow Church teaching through continence or natural family planning would grow in love for their spouses, gain mastery over their sexual appetites, and strengthen their marriages. Those predictions, too, have come to pass. Catholic marriages that observe Church teaching have an extremely low divorce rate.

Following the instructions of the pope ensures that you live the fullness of the Catholic faith, expressed through the sacraments, which strengthen your bonds to Christ and his universal Church.

Praying for the Pope

Exodus tells the story of a battle between the Israelites and an Amalekite army. Moses told Joshua to fight while he, Aaron, and Hur stood on a hill and prayed as the battle raged. Moses prayed with his hands upraised. As long as his arms were raised, Israel gained ground; but when Moses lowered his arms, the Amalekites gained the advantage. As Moses' arms grew tired, Aaron and Hur made him sit down and they supported his arms. As a result, Israel won the battle (Ex 17:8–13).

The story illustrates that leaders need prayer support. The Church is locked in a daily battle against the world, the flesh, and the devil, and the pope is interceding to God for the Church. But he needs the prayer support of all the faithful, holding his arms up in prayer, as it were. The greater the responsibility of the leader, the more prayer and support he needs. Pointing to this story from Exodus, the *Catechism* explains that prayer itself is a battle (*CCC* 2573–74), and the pope can't fight it alone. Prayer changes circumstances and changes the hearts of those who pray. The Church, along with the pope, must be committed to the spiritual battle (cf. 2 Cor 10:3–4; Eph 6:10–18).

The Exodus story also illustrates the need for *constant* prayer. Each day, the Church prays for the pope's intentions, which address the welfare of the Church all over the world. But more is needed. Catholics need to pray for the bishops he appoints because, as successors to the apostles, they teach, govern, and sanctify locally as the pope does universally. What's more, one of the bishops is likely to become the next pope. And, when the Chair of Peter becomes vacant, the Church should be engaged in prayer for the election of a successor who will faithfully serve in the present age. The faithful will then need to step forward in prayer to support the arms of that pope.

APPENDIX 1

Chronological List of the Popes

1. St. Peter, d. 67
2. St. Linus, 67–76
3. St. Anacletus, 76–88
4. St. Clement I, 88–96
5. St. Evaristus, 97–105
6. St. Alexander I, 105–115
7. St. Sixtus (Xystus) I, 115–125
8. St. Telesphorus, 125–136
9. St. Hyginus, 136–140
10. St. Pius I, 140–155
11. St. Anicetus, 155–166
12. St. Soter, 166–175
13. St. Eleutherius, 175–189
14. St. Victor I, 189–199
15. St. Zephyrinus, 199–217
16. St. Callistus I, 217–222
17. St. Urban I, 222–230
18. St. Pontian, 230–235
19. St. Anterus, 235–236
20. St. Fabian, 236–250
21. St. Cornelius, 251–253
22. St. Lucius I, 253–254
23. St. Stephen I, 254–257
24. St. Sixtus (Xystus) II, 257–258
25. St. Dionysius, 259–268

26. St. Felix I, 269–274
27. St. Eutychian, 275–283
28. St. Caius, 283–296
29. St. Marcellinus, 296–304
30. St. Marcellus I, 308–309
31. St. Eusebius, 309 (310)
32. St. Melchiades (Miltiades), 311–314
33. St. Sylvester I, 314–335
34. St. Marcus, 336
35. St. Julius I, 337–352
36. Liberius, 352–366
37. St. Damasus I, 366–384
38. St. Siricius, 384–399
39. St. Anastasius I, 399–401
40. St. Innocent I, 401–417
41. St. Zosimus, 417–418
42. St. Boniface I, 418–422
43. St. Celestine I, 422–432
44. St. Sixtus (Xystus) III, 432–440
45. St. Leo I (the Great), 440–461
46. St. Hilarus, 461–468
47. St. Simplicius, 468–483
48. St. Felix III (II), 483–492
49. St. Gelasius I, 492–496

50. St. Anastasius II, 496–498
51. St. Symmachus, 498–514
52. St. Hormisdas, 514–523
53. St. John I, 523–526
54. St. Felix IV/III, 526–530
55. Boniface II, 530–532
56. John II, 533–535
57. St. Agapetus I, 535–536
58. St. Silverius, 536–537
59. Vigilius, 537–555
60. Pelagius I, 556–561
61. John III, 561–574
62. Benedict I, 575–579
63. Pelagius II, 579–590
64. St. Gregory I, 590–604
65. Sabinianus, 604–606
66. Boniface III, 607
67. St. Boniface IV, 608–615
68. St. Deusdedit 615–618
69. Boniface V, 619–625
70. Honorius I, 625–638
71. Severinus, 640
72. John IV, 640–642
73. Theodore I, 642–649
74. St. Martin I, 649–655
75. St. Eugene I, 654–657
76. St. Vitalian, 657–672
77. Adeodatus, 672–676
78. Donus, 676–678
79. St. Agatho, 678–681
80. St. Leo II, 682–683
81. St. Benedict II, 684–685
82. John V, 685–686
83. Conon, 686–687
84. St. Sergius I, 687–701
85. John VI, 701–705
86. John VII, 705–707

87. Sisinnius, 708
88. Constantine, 708–715
89. St. Gregory II, 715–731
90. St. Gregory III, 731–741
91. St. Zachary, 741–752
Stephen II 752 (elected but
died before his consecration)
92. Stephen II (III), 752–
    757
93. St. Paul I, 757–767
94. Stephen III (IV), 768–
    772
95. Adrian I, 772–795
96. St. Leo III, 795–816
97. Stephen IV (V) 816–817
98. St. Paschal I, 817–824
99. Eugene II, 824–827
100. Valentine, 827
101. Gregory IV, 827–844
102. Sergius II, 844–847
103. St. Leo IV, 847–855
104. Benedict III, 855–858
105. St. Nicholas I (the
     Great), 858–867
106. Adrian II, 867–872
107. John VIII, 872–882
108. Marinus I (Martin II),
     882–884
109. Adrian III, 884–885
110. Stephen V (VI), 885–
     891
111. Formosus, 891–896
112. Boniface VI, 896
113. Stephen VI (VII), 896–
     897
114. Romanus, 897
115. Theodore II, 897

116. John IX, 898–900

117. Benedict IV, 900–903

118. Leo V, 903

119. Sergius III, 904–911

120. Anastasius III, 911–913

121. Landus, 913–914

122. John X, 914–928

123. Leo VI, 928

124. Stephen VII (VIII), 928–931

125. John XI, 931–936

126. Leo VII, 936–939

127. Stephen VIII (IX), 939–942

128. Marinus II (Martin III), 942–946

129. Agapetus II, 946–955

130. John XII, 955–964

131. Leo VIII, 963–965

132. Benedict V, 964–966

133. John XIII, 965–972

134. Benedict VI, 973–974

135. Benedict VII, 974–983

136. John XIV, 983–984

137. John XV, 985–996

138. Gregory V, 996–999

139. Silvester II, 999–1003

140. John XVII, 1003

141. John XVIII, 1004–1009

142. Sergius IV, 1009–1012

143. Benedict VIII, 1012–1024

144. John XIX, 1024–1032

145. Benedict IX, 1032–1044

146. Silvester III, 1045

147. Benedict IX, 1045

148. Gregory VI, 1045–1046

149. Clement 11, 1046–1047

150. Benedict IX, 1047–1048

151. Damasus II, 1048

152. St. Leo IX, 1049–1054

153. Victor II, 1055–1057

154. Stephen IX (X), 1057–1058

155. Nicholas II, 1059–1061

156. Alexander II, 1061–1073

157. St. Gregory VII, 1073–1085

158. Bl. Victor III, 1086–1087

159. Bl. Urban II, 1088–1099

160. Paschal II, 1099–1118

161. Gelasius II, 1118–1119

162. Callistus II, 1119–1124

163. Honorius II, 1124–1130

164. Innocent II, 1130–1143

165. Celestine II, 1143–1144

166. Lucius II, 1144–1145

167. Bl. Eugene III, 1145–1153

168. Anastasius IV, 1153–1154

169. Adrian IV, 1154–1159

170. Alexander III, 1159–1181

171. Lucius III, 1181–1185

172. Urban III, 1185–1187

173. Gregory VIII, 1187

174. Clement III, 1187–1191

175. Celestine III, 1191–1198

176. Innocent III, 1198–1216

177. Honorius III, 1216–1227

178. Gregory IX, 1227–1241
179. Celestine IV, 1241
180. Innocent IV, 1243–1254
181. Alexander IV, 1254–1261
182. Urban IV, 1261–1264
183. Clement IV, 1265–1268
184. Bl. Gregory X, 1271–1276
185. Bl. Innocent V, 1276
186. Adrian V, 1276
187. John XXI, 1276–1277
188. Nicholas III, 1277–1280
189. Martin IV, 1281–1285
190. Honorius IV, 1285–1287
191. Nicholas IV, 1288–1292
192. St. Celestine V, 1294
193. Boniface VIII, 1294–1303
194. Bl. Benedict XI, 1303–1304
195. Clement V, 1305–1314
196. John XXII, 1316–1334
197. Benedict XII, 1334–1342
198. Clement VI, 1342–1352
199. Innocent VI, 1352–1362
200. Bl. Urban V, 1362–1370
201. Gregory XI, 1370–1378
202. Urban VI, 1378–1389
203. Boniface IX, 1389–1404
204. Innocent VII, 1404–1406
205. Gregory XII, 1406–1415
206. Martin V, 1417–1431
207. Eugene IV, 1431–1447
208. Nicholas V, 1447–1455
209. Callistus III, 1455–1458
210. Pius II, 1458–1464
211. Paul II, 1464–1471
212. Sixtus IV, 1471–1484
213. Innocent VIII, 1484–1492
214. Alexander VI, 1492–1503
215. Pius III, 1503
216. Julius II, 1503–1513
217. Leo X, 1513–1521
218. Adrian VI, 1522–1523
219. Clement VII, 1523–1534
220. Paul III, 1534–1549
221. Julius III, 1550–1555
222. Marcellus II, 1555
223. Paul IV, 1555–1559
224. Pius IV, 1559–1565
225. St. Pius V, 1566–1572
226. Gregory XIII, 1572–1585
227. Sixtus V, 1585–1590
228. Urban VII, 1590
229. Gregory XIV, 1590–1591
230. Innocent IX, 1591
231. Clement VIII, 1592–1605
232. Leo XI, 1605
233. Paul V, 1605–1621
234. Gregory XV, 1621–1623
235. Urban VIII, 1623–1644
236. Innocent X, 1644–1655

237. Alexander VII, 1655–1667
238. Clement IX, 1667–1669
239. Clement X, 1670–1676
240. Bl. Innocent XI, 1676–1689
241. Alexander VIII, 1689–1691
242. Innocent XII, 1691–1700
243. Clement XI, 1700–1721
244. Innocent XIII, 1721–1724
245. Benedict XIII, 1724–1730
246. Clement XII, 1730–1740
247. Benedict XIV, 1740–1758
248. Clement XIII, 1758–1769
249. Clement XIV, 1769–1774

250. Pius VI, 1775–1799
251. Pius VII, 1800–1823
252. Leo XII, 1823–1829
253. Pius VIII, 1829–1830
254. Gregory XVI, 1831–1846
255. Bl. Pius IX, 1846–1878
256. Leo XIII, 1878–1903
257. St. Pius X, 1903–1914
258. Benedict XV, 1914–1922
259. Pius XI, 1922–1939
260. Pius XII, 1939–1958
261. St. John XXIII, 1958–1963
262. Bl. Paul VI, 1963–1978
263. John Paul I, 1978
264. St. John Paul II, 1978–2005
265. Benedict XVI, 2005–2013
266. Francis, 2013–

APPENDIX 2

A Short Glossary

cardinal: A high-ranking prelate and advisor to the pope. The name comes from the Latin word for "hinge" (*cardo*). Today, the College of Cardinals elects the pope when the office becomes vacant.

charism: A gift given by the Holy Spirit to the Church as a whole or to an individual on behalf of the whole Church.

church: A convocation or assembly, specifically a Christian assembly, whether the universal Church of all Catholics united with the successor of Peter or a local church of Christians united with a validly ordained bishop.

collegiality: The exercise of authority or responsibility by all members of a group.

conclave: A closed meeting of the College of Cardinals to elect a pope.

definition: In a doctrinal context, a statement that brings to an end any legitimate dispute about a matter. Often used by the Church's Magisterium in settling matters of faith and morals.

doctrine: A teaching.

ecumenical council: A general council or meeting of the bishops of the world. For its decrees to be binding, they must be confirmed by the Roman Pontiff.

ecumenism: A movement whose goal is to promote unity among Christians.

encyclical: A teaching document written in the form of a letter.

ex cathedra: (Latin, "from the chair [of Peter]") A phrase indicating a statement of the highest authority made when the pope exercises the fullness of his teaching office to define a matter concerning faith or morals to be believed by all the faithful. *Ex cathedra* statements are infallible.

excommunication: The act of excluding someone from membership in the Church.

heresy: The obstinate postbaptismal doubt or denial of a truth that must be believed with divine and Catholic faith.

Holy See: The see of Rome. ("See" refers to the bishop's "seat" of authority; in this case, the pope's.)

impeccability: Inability to sin.

infallibility: The inability to err in matters of faith or morals—a charism given to the Church, in which the pope participates.

inspiration: The movement of the Holy Spirit by which the Scriptures were "breathed by God".

Magisterium: The teaching office of the Church consisting of the pope and the bishops teaching in union with him.

patriarch: A bishop who governs a major portion of the Church, such as a ritual church or a large territory. The pope is the patriarch of the West.

pontiff: Literally, a bridge builder; a title of the pope as a representative of Christ.

pope: "Father"; a title reserved within the Catholic Church to the bishop of Rome by Leo I.

primacy: The highest level of authority among all those of similar rank.

Tradition: The handing down of the faith of the apostles, in oral or written (scriptural) form.

APPENDIX 3

Recommended Citations of Scripture and the *Catechism of the Catholic Church*

Scripture	New Testament	Lk 10:16
		Lk 22:31–32
Old Testament	Mt 5–7 (all)	
	Mt 5:48	Jn 1:42
Gen 45:4	Mt 6:7, 13	Jn 6 (all)
	Mt 8:10	Jn 12:3–5
Ex 13:3	Mt 13:31–32	Jn 13:14–15
Ex 17:8–13	Mt 14:30	Jn 14:6, 25
Ex 20:19	Mt 16:17–19	Jn 16:8–11, 13–18
Ex 23:10	Mt 17:1	Jn 17:21–23
Ex 25–28 (all)	Mt 18:18	Jn 20:23, 30–31
	Mt 22:21	Jn 21:15–17,
Lev 26:12	Mt 26:35	18–19, 25
	Mt 28:18–20	
Num 16 (all)		Acts 1:15–22
Num 27:15–23	Mk 5:37	Acts 2 (all)
	Mk 6:7–13	Acts 2:41–42, 44
Deut 18:4, 15–19	Mk 9:2	Acts 2:14–42, 44
	Mk 10:43–45	Acts 3 (all)
1 Chron 22 (all)	Mk 14:33	Acts 4:12, 32–34,
1 Chron 28–29 (all)		41
	Lk 2:52	Acts 4:32–5:11,
Is 22:20–23	Lk 5:1–11	14
	Lk 4:38–39	Acts 5:1–11
Jer 7:23	Lk 8:51	Acts 5:12, 14
	Lk 9:28	
Ezek 36:28		
Mal 1:6–9		

Acts 5:15–16
Acts 5:42
Acts 6 (all)
Acts 6:1–7
Acts 8:14–24
Acts 9:1–2, 32–43
Acts 10 (all)
Acts 10:1–11, 18
Acts 10:47–48
Acts 11 (all)
Acts 11:1–18
Acts 12:1–5, 17
Acts 14:23
Acts 15 (all)
Acts 15:5–12, 15–22, 28
Acts 16:18
Acts 23:5

Rom 1:11, 17–21
Rom 2:14–15
Rom 10:14, 17
Rom 12:5

1 Cor 1:10
1 Cor 2:16
1 Cor 3:11
1 Cor 12:7

2 Cor 5:18–20
2 Cor 10:3–6

Gal 2:2, 6–10, 11–21

Eph 1:10
Eph 2:20
Eph 4:5
Eph 6:10–18

Col 4:16

1 Tim 1:5
1 Tim 3:15
1 Tim 4:6–16
1 Tim 6:20

2 Tim 1:7
2 Tim 2:1–2
2 Tim 3:15, 16

1 Pet 1:1
1 Pet 2:9
1 Pet 5:1–3, 12

2 Pet 1:12–15
2 Pet 1:16–2:1
2 Pet 3:8, 11–14, 15–17

Rev 19:6–9
Rev 21:14

Catechism of the Catholic Church
(numbers refer to paragraph numbers, not pages)

66
105–8
171
553
751

801
820
830
838–39
841

843–46
880–82
891–92
2573–74

APPENDIX 4

Where to Learn More

Key Works

The following are standard references for anyone seeking to understand Catholic teaching on the papacy.

Catechism of the Catholic Church: Second Edition. Washington, D.C.: Libreria Editrice Vaticana—United States Conference of Catholic Bishops, 2000. [This volume has a glossary of terms and several valuable indexes.]

The Holy Bible: Revised Standard Version; Second Catholic Edition. San Francisco: Ignatius Press, 2006.

Vatican Council II, Vol. 1: The Conciliar and Post Conciliar Documents. Edited by Austin Flannery, O.P. Northport, N.Y.: Costello Publishing, 1987. [The Dogmatic Constitution on the Church *Lumen Gentium* presents the core teaching. The older Abbott translation sometimes is clearer, but is less readily available and contains some translation problems.]

Recommended Reading

Bokenkotter, Thomas K. *A Concise History of the Catholic Church.* New York: Doubleday Image Books, 1990. [This is a revised and expanded edition of this author's popular one-volume history of the Church.]

Hughes, John Jay. *Pontiffs: Popes Who Shaped History*. Huntington, Ind.: Our Sunday Visitor Publishing, 1994. [Portraits of eleven significant popes who "made a difference" in the history of the papal office. Written during the pontificate of John Paul II, the book, however, says nothing about his reign.]

Kelly, J. N. D. *The Oxford Dictionary of Popes*. New York: Oxford University Press, 1986. [The lives of the popes are arranged in chronological order. Because it is a biographical dictionary, the book does not present much information about the historical backgrounds in which the popes lived and worked. The author is a Protestant, but still provides valuable information.]

Madrid, Patrick. *Pope Fiction: Answers to 30 Myths & Misconceptions about the Papacy*. Rancho Santa Fe, Calif.: Basilica Press, 2000. [Very readable by a popular audience, the book is a must for answering common objections to the papacy.]

Miller, J. Michael, C.S.B. *The Shepherd and the Rock: Origins, Development, and Mission of the Papacy*. Huntington, Ind.: Our Sunday Visitor Publishing, 1995. [This book discusses in detail many aspects of the papacy.]

Ray, Stephen K. *Upon This Rock: St. Peter and the Primacy of Rome in Scripture and the Early Church*. San Francisco: Ignatius Press, 1999. [This valuable book gathers together the scriptural and main texts from the early Church Fathers, and discusses the history of the development of the early papacy.]

Ray, Stephen K. *Peter, Keeper of the Keys*. The Footprints of God (DVD series). Fort Collins, CO: Ignatius Press, 2003.

SUBJECT INDEX

acclamation, selection of pope
 by, 96, 97, 101
Ad Gentes (1965), 118n16
ad limina apostolorum visits, 30
Ad Petri Cathedram (1959),
 103n1
Albigensianism, 32, 82*b*
Alexander I (pope), 96
Ananias, 24
Anglicanorum Coetibus (2009),
 111
Anglicans, 110–11
anti-Catholic attacks. *See*
 attacks on papacy
antipopes, 74*b*, 125
anti-Semitism, 42–43, 103,
 112–13
apostolic constitutions, 56
apostolic exhortations, 56–57
Arius and Arianism, 32, 33
Assumption of Mary, 15, 15*b*,
 56
Assyrian Church of the East, 36
Athenagoras I (Orthodox
 patriarch), 36, 44, 108
attacks on papacy, 119–27
 antipopes breaking line of
 succession from Peter,
 125
 doctrine, ability of pope to
 change, 119–20

government leader and head
 of state, pope as, 126–27
incorrect statements made by
 popes, 120–21
infallibility issues, 120–21
James as head of Jerusalem
 church, 124
Jews in WWII, accusations
 against Pius XII
 regarding, 42–43, 113
Paul regarded as chief
 apostle, 123–24
on Peter as foundation of
 Church, 121–22
Peter rebuked by Paul,
 122–23
riches of papacy not used to
 support the poor, 125–26
sinfulness of popes, 121
Attila the Hun, 77–78
Augustine of Canterbury, 41, 81

baptism, 11, 12, 22, 27, 38–39
Benedict XIV (pope), 52
Benedict XVI (pope), 29n4,
 31, 92, 98, 99, 102, 110–11,
 113, 133
Bergoglio, Jorge. *See* Francis
Bible. *See* Scripture Index
birth control, 16, 18, 48, 49*b*,
 131, 134

Page numbers followed by an italic *b* indicate box features.

SCRIPTURE INDEX